RAND ARROYO CENTER

How Deployments Affect the Capacity and Utilization of Army Treatment Facilities

Adam C. Resnick, Mireille Jacobson, Srikanth Kadiyala,
Nicole K. Eberhart, Susan D. Hosek

Prepared for the United States Army

Approved for public release; distribution unlimited

The research described in this report was sponsored by the United States
Army under Contract No. W74V8H-06-C-0001.

Library of Congress Cataloging-in-Publication Data is available for this
publication.

ISBN 978-0-8330-8045-5

The RAND Corporation is a nonprofit institution that helps improve policy
and decisionmaking through research and analysis. RAND's publications do
not necessarily reflect the opinions of its research clients and sponsors.

Support RAND—make a tax-deductible charitable contribution at
www.rand.org/giving/contribute.html

RAND® is a registered trademark

RAND OFFICES
SANTA MONICA, CA • WASHINGTON, DC
PITTSBURGH, PA • NEW ORLEANS, LA • JACKSON, MS • BOSTON, MA
CAMBRIDGE, UK • BRUSSELS, BE
www.rand.org

Preface

Over the course of the Overseas Contingency Operations, the U.S. Army has sustained a deployment of well over 100,000 soldiers. To continue to generate these deployable forces, the Army instituted the Army Force Generation (ARFORGEN) cycle. This cycle established a repeating process by which Army units would reset and train, and be ready and available to deploy. The cycle was designed to make the process of generating deployable units more predictable, but the Army was concerned that it did not fully understand how the process would affect the lives of Army soldiers and families. The Vice Chief of Staff of the Army (VCSA) asked RAND Arroyo Center to investigate collateral effects of deployment cycle events. In a response to the VCSA's request, Arroyo launched five projects, including this one, investigating outcomes of the way the Army was deploying forces, beyond the deliberately instilled unit cycle. This project is titled "Army Medical Department (AMEDD) Beneficiaries Health Care Needs, Deployment Cycle Effects."

This report is intended for audiences in the military health system, who may appreciate learning how deployments affect military treatment facilities and health care beneficiaries, and audiences interested in health policy research, who may gain a greater understanding of how families under stress utilize care.

This research was sponsored by the Army Surgeon General (TSG) and conducted within RAND Arroyo Center's Army Health Program. The action officer is the Office of The Surgeon General, Program Analysis and Evaluation (OTSG PA&E).

The Project Unique Identification Code (PUIC) for the project that produced this document is ASPMO09461. The principal investigator, Adam Resnick, can be reached by email at Adam_Resnick@rand.org; by phone at 310-393-0411, extension 6027; or by mail at The RAND Corporation, 1776 Main Street, Santa Monica, California, 90407.

For more information on RAND Arroyo Center, contact the Director of Operations (telephone 310-393-0411, extension 6419; fax 310-451-6952; email Marcy_Agmon@rand.org), or visit Arroyo's website at http://www.rand.org/ard.html.

Contents

Figures

Table

Summary

Ongoing deployments since 2004 have affected the population dynamics at military installations and military treatment facilities (MTFs). When operational Army units such as infantry brigades deploy, active-duty health care providers assigned to the units go with them, and so do some active-duty providers who are assigned to work full-time at MTFs. So when large Army units deploy and leave the installations at which they train, the number of providers available to provide care for soldiers and other beneficiaries at the installation decreases, as does the number of beneficiaries seeking care, through the large-scale departure of soldiers deploying with the units. Under the Army Force Generation (ARFORGEN) cycle, units and large numbers of soldiers deploy and return home to installations on a predictable schedule, and during the affected time periods, the population of the installation shifts (e.g., resulting in fewer soldiers present or a changing mix of soldiers).

Army officials were concerned about the possible effects of variations (driven by deployments) on the demand for and availability of health care. In particular, the Vice Chief of Staff of the Army (VCSA) wanted to know whether Army deployments were having unintended and unknown effects on the well-being of soldiers and their immediate families. The VCSA was concerned that ebbs and flows in the ability of Army military treatment facilities to provide medical care might affect the system's ability to respond to changes in family needs as soldiers deploy, redeploy, and return home.

In March 2009, the VCSA asked RAND Arroyo Center to investigate the "collateral effects" of ARFORGEN on soldiers' and, especially, families' ability to receive health care. Aware of the deployment cycle changes in the number of available health care providers and beneficiaries seeking care, we were also cognizant of recent military health research showing that the family members of service members who deployed utilized health care in different ways (Eide et al., 2010; McNulty, 2003; Gorman et al., 2010). We designed a study to focus on two main questions:

- How does the deployment cycle affect capacity and beneficiary utilization at *Army MTFs*?
- How does the deployment cycle affect *family* health care utilization?

To answer the first question, we performed an aggregate-level analysis of deployment cycle effects on installations. This analysis included 14 installations, which accounted for 80 percent of the soldier deployments in the time period of our analysis, 2004–2009. To answer the second question, we performed a longitudinal analysis of Army families to identify how individual family utilization changes when members of the family deploy (while controlling for other factors). To perform this analysis, we assembled longitudinal records for Army family members, linking all TRICARE-eligible beneficiaries to the sponsoring active component soldier and including available demographic data for family members (age, gender, ethnicity). This analysis included the majority of the overseas contingency operations spanning 2004–2009, and the majority of active component family members who are enrolled in TRICARE Prime.

MTF-Level Analysis of Deployment Cycle Effects

We performed an analysis of 14 installations in the United States that deploy brigade combat teams (BCTs), the fundamental unit of Army deployments, and host Army hospitals. These installations are not typical military installations—they are the specific Army forts that deploy the vast majority of forces, and are referred to as force projection platforms. Over the course of this analysis, these installations generated 80 percent of deploying soldiers.[1] This analysis investigated changes in: beneficiary population at installations, capacity at installation MTFs, utilization at the MTF from civilian providers, and MTF provider workload.

We hypothesized that if large numbers of soldiers deployed concurrently, the dramatically diminished population of beneficiaries remaining nearby to the installations would utilize less care, in aggregate. We also expected that the total number of health care providers available at installations would decrease when Army units deployed, in that MTFs would not bring in military, civilian, or contractor providers in sufficient quantity to offset the loss. However, we did not know which change would be larger proportionally, the decrease in providers or in beneficiaries.

We hypothesized that access to care would change when the number of providers available and the number of beneficiaries competing for appointments changed, and that families of deploying soldiers might change the way they sought care. However, we did not know whether access to care would increase or decrease, and how families would seek care differently. So we could not project what changes related to access and care-seeking behavior we would observe in utilization by the beneficiaries (dependents and nondeploying soldiers) remaining near installations when Army units deployed.

Effects of Soldier Deployment on Beneficiary Population and Enrollment at the MTF

At the 14 installations in our analysis, we quantified the changes in beneficiary population sizes for the following groups: soldiers enrolled at the MTFs, who may deploy; soldier family members enrolled for care with the MTFs and with civilian network providers, who may leave the area when soldiers deploy; and, to a limited extent, retirees and their dependents who enrolled at MTFs for care, whose needs we

---

[1]   In the Army, deployable combat units are staffed by a greater proportion of junior enlisted soldiers than other types of units are, and so the installations in this analysis house a population of soldiers who are slightly younger and have slightly fewer dependents than the Army-wide demographic.

do not expect to change related to the deployment cycle. The size of the beneficiary population is a main driver of the overall demand for care, compounded with the rate at which beneficiaries utilize care.

Soldiers account for approximately 40 percent of MTF enrollees, which is equivalent to soldier family members, who account for approximately 40 percent of MTF enrollees. Retirees and their dependents make up the balance, or approximately 20 percent of enrollees at the MTF. We present these data as a basic context to understand the extent to which changes in utilization by each group will affect overall utilization.[2]

Nearly all soldiers who enroll with TRICARE enroll at the MTF for care. We study changes in the enrolled soldier population and changes in the health care this population utilizes. However, we also observe that nonenrolled soldiers account for a sizable amount of care at MTFs. From discussions with MTF staff, we understand that soldiers who are temporarily assigned to an installation for training are not enrolled at the MTF. We expect that these trainees generate many of the visits by nonenrolled soldiers, but we do not study this population. Whether these visits are generated by trainees or other nonenrolled soldiers does not affect our analysis. Although we cannot quantify the nonenrolled soldier population that relies upon the MTF for care in our analysis data, we do include MTF visits by these soldiers in the analysis, as changes in these visits may magnify or more likely mitigate effects from deploying soldiers.

Over the course of the analysis, the population of beneficiaries grew, and the portion of soldiers enrolled at the MTFs grew. While the population of soldiers enrolled at MTFs in our analysis grew from 229,000 to 314,000,[3] the population of family members enrolled at MTFs increased slightly less, from 292,000 to 319,000. During this time there was a large increase in family members enrolled at network

---

[2]   As soldier populations grew at the installations over the course of the analysis, soldiers grew to represent a slightly larger percentage of the beneficiaries enrolled at the MTFs.

[3]   When soldiers deploy, they do not change their enrollment status. We identify when soldiers deploy through other elements in their personnel data designed for this purpose.

providers at the installations in our analysis, an increase from 49,000 to 95,000.

Soldier deployments had major effects on the population in-garrison at the installations in our analysis. Most installations saw as many as 60 percent of the assigned soldiers deploy concurrently, emptying out the installation. We attempted to discern the extent to which soldier families left installations when units deployed but could not do so conclusively. We observe sizable changes in the population of family members living near and enrolled at MTFs, but some changes appear to be broad patterns of growth or reduction, and it is difficult to observe a clear relationship between population changes and deployments. Additionally, we note that families may not reliably update addresses and TRICARE enrollment if they move from the area temporarily.

Effects of Deployment on Health Care Provider Availability

To understand the effects of deployments on installations, we considered how deployments affect the number of providers at MTFs, the quantity of provider full-time equivalent (FTE) hours available for patient care, and provider workload.

Over the period studied (2004–2009), there was a change in the mix of providers at MTFs that was steady and not specifically related to the deployment cycle. In 2004, nearly three-fourths of the FTEs at the MTFs in the analysis were active-duty, with the largest represented group being active-duty physicians. By 2009, civilian and contractor providers accounted for nearly half of the FTEs at the MTFs, and the fastest-growing group consisted of civilian and contractor providers other than physicians, particularly civilian mental health and primary care professionals.

Providers Assigned to MTFs Typically Do Not Deploy in Large Numbers When Installation Soldiers Deploy

We observed a strong relationship between soldier deployments and deployment of health care providers assigned to the operational units (table of organization and equipment, or TOE, providers), but a weak relationship between soldier deployments and deployment of the health care providers assigned to the MTFs (table of distribution and allowances, or TDA, providers). In the 14 installations in our analysis, TDA providers assigned to MTFs did not typically deploy in significant numbers when soldiers from the same installation deployed. In contrast, TOE providers, who are generally battalion surgeons and physician assistants (PAs), deployed nearly in parallel with soldiers from the same installations. A large unit deploying from an installation may cause a decrease in the at-home soldier population by 40 percent.[4] Using that as an example, when 40 percent of the soldiers at an installation deploy, only about 2 percent of providers assigned to the MTF deploy, while 32 percent of providers assigned to the installation's operational units deploy.

These effects varied across installations. "Purer" deployment platforms such as Fort Stewart, whose primary focus is to deploy units, experienced a more noticeable surge in TDA provider deployments when soldiers deployed, while Fort Bragg, which has missions other than deploying troops and a medical center instead of a community hospital, experienced little if any effect of deployments on TDA providers in-garrison at the local MTF.

There Was a Small Effect on Available Patient Care Hours When Soldiers Deployed

We observed a similarly weak relationship between soldier deployments and FTEs for civilian, contractor, and active-duty providers at MTFs. When 40 percent of the soldiers are deployed from an installation, we observed approximately 5 percent fewer outpatient-care FTEs from active-duty, civilian, and contractor providers available at the MTF than would be available if all soldiers were in-garrison. We did not observe a statistically significant change in the sum of patient-care FTEs and nonpatient-care FTEs at MTFs when soldiers deployed. In other words, when soldiers deployed, total provider FTEs at the MTFs did not change significantly, and outpatient-care FTEs decreased only slightly. We infer from these results that there is a weak relationship between patient-care FTEs recorded at Army MTFs and deployments.

---

[4] 40 percent of enrolled soldiers deploying is approximately the median effect at an installation in our analysis when a BCT or larger soldier population deploys.

Beneficiary Utilization of Health Care Across the Deployment Cycle

We examined the amount of health care utilized by beneficiaries (soldiers, families, retirees) across the deployment cycle. We looked at the mix of care from MTFs and civilian network providers utilized by beneficiaries to see whether there are changes during the deployment cycle.

We first describe the broader trends in Army beneficiary health care utilization before studying effects specifically related to the deployment cycle.

The Rate of Beneficiary Utilization of Health Care Increased 10 Percent over the Period Studied

Over the time period of the analysis, the rate of utilization grew approximately 10 percent in all categories: soldier and family member, MTF-enrolled or network-enrolled. On average, soldiers utilized health care resources at approximately twice the rate of family members. This finding is not surprising. Soldiers are required to visit a provider to receive permission to stay home from work and are not allowed to self-prescribe bed-rest for minor conditions, as civilians are. When soldiers attend sick call in an MTF clinic, these visits are recorded as utilization in the electronic medical record and appear in the data used in our analysis.

Families of soldiers at the installations in our analysis enrolled to both the MTFs and to civilian network providers for primary care. Families enrolled to the MTF got the majority of their care from the MTF, but still received 15 percent of their care from civilian providers. Family members enrolled to civilian providers received two-thirds of their care from civilian providers, and one-third from MTFs. We did not perform any analysis to understand differences in these populations, as it was outside the bounds of our analysis, but we did observe that family members enrolled to MTFs utilize 65 percent more care than family members enrolled to civilian providers.

Deployments Were Associated with an Increase in In-Garrison Soldier MTF Visits, but No Consistent Effect on Aggregate Utilization by Families

When soldiers deployed, soldier MTF visits decreased, although at a lesser rate than the decrease in soldier population in-garrison at the installation. When operational units deploy, we observed in our analysis that soldier visits decrease in one-third proportion to the deploying soldiers. For example, when 40 percent of the soldiers at an installation deploy, we observe that soldier visits to the MTF decrease by 13 percent. When soldiers deploy, soldiers who remain in-garrison use care at a higher rate than the overall soldier population.

We do not observe a statistically significant change in aggregate outpatient care at the MTFs by the populations of family members, or retirees and their dependents, when soldiers deploy.

Health Care Utilization Per-Provider Decreased When Soldiers Deploy

Although there was a slight decrease in the quantity of patient-care FTEs generated at MTFs when soldiers deploy, the rate of patient visits per provider FTE decreased during deployments. For example, when 40 percent of the soldiers from an installation are deployed, we observe outpatient workload per provider FTE to be approximately 5 percent lower across all types of visits.

Individual-Level Analysis of Family Health Care Utilization

We performed a longitudinal analysis of health care utilization by soldier family members. This analysis builds on a significant body of research defining how stress affects families, and how deployments affect family health care utilization. Our analysis extends the current body of research in several key ways: we analyzed care utilized by soldier family members at civilian providers as well as MTFs; we extended beyond regular outpatient care to look at ER and pharmacy utilization; we used statistical methods that control for other factors that may influence health care utilization; and we performed an analysis that looked at how the experience of individuals changed when a soldier deployed from their own family. Other studies that investigated effects of deployment on families have typically selected a short time horizon and compared the utilization by two distinct populations, those family members who have soldiers deploying, and those who do not. In our research we will be able to define the effects of deployment with more certainty, having controlled for other factors.

Spouse Utilization

We studied the changes in health care utilization by soldier spouses. We saw that spouses decrease their utilization of outpatient care by 8 percent when soldiers in their family deploy. We were very interested to see that utilization at MTFs actually decreased by a greater amount, by 12 percent. Spouses changed their behaviors, and utilized more care from civilian providers, as outpatient care from civilian providers increased by 3 percent.

In our discussions with the Army medical community, they indicated their perception that family members tended to move from the area when soldiers in their families deployed. We designed an analysis to observe changes in outpatient care utilization from civilian providers who were located within 40 miles of the MTFs, and those located outside the area.[5] We saw that while spouse utilization at civilian providers increased 3 percent overall, it actually decreased by 4 percent within 40 miles of the MTF, and increased by 35 percent at providers outside a 40-mile radius of the MTF. From this finding we conclude that spouses are indeed leaving the area when soldiers in their families deploy.

We studied mental health utilization by spouses. When soldiers in their families deployed, spouse utilization of total mental health care did not change much (increasing by 0.1 percent), but spouses were 4 percent more likely to visit for diagnoses related to mood, adjustment, and anxiety.[6] These diagnoses are used commonly in health care research to define symptoms of stress and depression.

---

[5]   We chose 40 miles as a definition of the area surrounding an MTF, since the military uses the same distance to define the population of beneficiaries to whom the MTF must be responsible for providing access to care.

[6]   During months when a soldier was not deployed, 48 percent of spouses utilized outpatient care, but only 6 percent of spouses utilized mental health care for the described diagnoses of mood, adjustment, and anxiety. So when we observed spouse utilization of mental health care for these diagnoses to increase relatively by 4 percent when soldiers deploy, in absolute terms the change was small.

Child Utilization

As we studied health care utilization by spouses when soldiers deployed, we performed a similar analysis of health care utilization by children. We saw that outpatient care for children did not change when soldiers deployed, but we saw a transfer in the source of care for children similar to what we saw for spouses. Children were 4 percent less likely to utilize outpatient care at MTFs, but were 1 percent more likely to utilize care at civilian providers.

We found the most dramatic changes in health care utilization when we studied children of custodial single parents.[7] These children must stay with an alternate caregiver when their parent deploys. We saw that children of custodial single parents were 15 percent less likely to utilize outpatient care when their parents deployed. They were 26 percent less likely to utilize care at MTFs, and 13 percent more likely to utilize care at civilian providers.

Pharmacy Utilization

When we studied pharmacy utilization by spouses and children, we saw that spouses were 7 percent less likely to use prescriptions when soldiers deployed, but they were 7 percent more likely to use prescriptions for antidepressants, which corresponds to our finding that spouses were more likely to utilize mental health care for stress- and depression-related diagnoses. Children were 1 percent more likely to utilize prescriptions, with increases in the likelihood of using antidepressants and anti-infectives.

Newer Army Families

In addition to studying all soldier family members enrolled in TRI-CARE Prime between 2004 and 2009, we performed an analysis of dependents of soldiers who joined the Army since 2001. It was our prediction that these families may experience greater deployment cycle

---

[7] In our analysis, 11 percent of the observations were of children of single, custodial parents. Children of two-parent households made up the predominance of observations in the analysis, and results for children of two-parent households are quite similar to those for the entire child population.

effects, having less experience in dealing with family stresses associated with deployments and in accessing health care through TRICARE and Army MTFs.

Beneficiaries in post-2001 Army families exhibited deployment cycle effects consistent with the whole Army population, but with notably larger effects. When soldiers deployed, effects on these Army families were 50–75 percent larger for the following primary outcomes: a decrease in MTF visits by spouses, children, and children of single parents; and an increase in civilian visits outside the local catchment area.

Conclusions

Our report resulted in the following conclusions:

- Soldier utilization decreases in aggregate with deployments, but nondeploying soldiers use more care during these times.
- MTF capacity is not greatly affected when soldiers deploy. In aggregate, family member access does not appear impinged when soldiers deploy, and MTFs may be slightly less busy.
- The deployment cycle affects installations differently. The portion of soldiers that deploy from an installation and the portion of providers that deploy from the MTF are two factors that vary across installations and can affect changes in the demand for care and availability of appointments at the MTF.
- Spouses and children of single parents were less likely to utilize care when soldiers deployed and were noticeably more likely to utilize care outside their area.
- All categories of family members shifted their care from MTFs to civilian providers.
- Spouses and children utilized more mental health care for stress- and depression-related diagnoses when soldiers in the family deployed. Spouses also increased utilization of antidepressants.

- Decreases in MTF utilization and increases in civilian care outside the catchment area were even greater for younger Army families.

Acknowledgments

The authors are grateful to LTG Eric B. Schoomaker, then the Army Surgeon General and Commanding General of Army Medical Command, and to LTG Patricia D. Horoho, the Army Surgeon General and Commanding General of Army Medical Command, for sponsoring the study. We thank COL Robert L. Goodman, then Director of Program Analysis and Evaluation, Office of the Surgeon General, and COL Patrick W. Grady, Director of Program Analysis and Evaluation, Office of the Surgeon General, for monitoring the study and providing constructive feedback during its course.

We are grateful for all the support we received from staff throughout the Army Medical Command, particularly the dedicated staff at Army military treatment facilities who met with us and provided valuable insight. We would also like to thank the soldiers and Army spouses who shared their experiences with us.

Thank you to our RAND colleagues Andrew Dick, Paco Martorell, and Michael Hansen for their thoughtful and thorough reviews of the manuscript.

Finally, at RAND, we wish to thank Margaret Harrell, the director of RAND Arroyo Center's Army Health Program, and Sarah Meadows, the associate director, for their insightful comments and assistance.

List of Acronyms

AMEDD	Army Medical Department
ARFORGEN	Army Force Generation
BCT	Brigade Combat Team
DEERS	Defense Enrollment Eligibility Reporting System
DMDC	Defense Manpower Data Center
ER	Emergency Room
FRAGO	Fragmentary Order
FTE	Full-Time Equivalent
HMO	Health Maintenance Organization
ID	Infantry Division
M2	MHS Management Analysis and Reporting Tool
MAA	Mood, Adjustment, or Anxiety
MEDCOM	Army Medical Command
MEPRS	Medical Expense and Performance Reporting System
MTF	Military Treatment Facility
OTSG PA&E	Office of The Surgeon General, Program Analysis and Evaluation
PA	Physician Assistant
PCM	Primary Care Manager
PDHA	Post-Deployment Health Assessment

PDHRA	Post-Deployment Health Re-Assessment
PHA	Periodic Health Assessment
PROFIS	Professional Filler System
RVU	Relative Value Unit
SADR	Standard Ambulatory Data Record
TDA	Table of Distribution and Allowances
TEDI	TRICARE Encounters Data Institutional
TEDNI	TRICARE Encounters Data Non-Institutional
TOE	Table of Organization and Equipment
TSG	The Surgeon General
UIC	Unit Identification Code
VCSA	Vice Chief Staff of the Army

CHAPTER ONE

Introduction

Ongoing deployments since 2004 have affected the population dynamics at military installations and military treatment facilities (MTFs). When operational Army units such as infantry brigades deploy, active-duty health care providers assigned to the units go with them, and so do some active-duty providers who are assigned to work full-time at MTFs. So when large Army units deploy and leave the installations at which they train, the number of providers available to provide care for soldiers and other beneficiaries at the installation decreases, as does the number of beneficiaries seeking care through the large-scale departure of soldiers deploying with the units. In the Army Force Generation (ARFORGEN) cycle, deployable Army units rotate through a cycle where they are either ready for deployment ("Available" phase), training intensively and eligible for deployment ("Train/Ready"), or returning from deployment ("Reset"). The cyclical nature of ARFORGEN means that large numbers of soldiers are leaving from or returning home to installations on a predictable schedule, and that, during some periods, the population of the installation shifts (e.g., resulting in fewer soldiers present or a changing mix of soldiers).

Army officials were concerned about the possible effects of cyclical variations in the demand for and availability of health services support. In particular, the Vice Chief of Staff of the Army (VCSA) asked whether Army deployments to support the overseas contingency operations were having unintended and unknown effects on the well-being of soldiers and their immediate families. The VCSA expressed concern that ebbs and flows in the ability of Army MTFs to provide medical care might not be attuned to the changes in family needs as soldiers prepare for deployment, deploy, and return home.

Health care for all beneficiaries of the Military Health System (MHS)—active-duty personnel, retired personnel, and dependents—is provided through the TRICARE program. TRICARE has two main options: Prime, a health maintenance organization (HMO) option that requires enrollment and a primary care manager (PCM), or Standard/ Extra, a preferred provider organization option that does not require enrollment or a PCM.[1] Prime enrollees are assigned to an MTF if possible,[2] or to a primary care physician from the TRICARE civilian provider network.

Prime enrollees seek primary care from their PCMs. When Prime enrollees are referred for specialty care, MTFs have the first opportunity to schedule the specialist appointments regardless of whether the referring PCM was at an MTF or civilian network facility. If MTFs do not have capacity to schedule specialty referrals, the referrals are routed to specialists at civilian network facilities.

Soldiers are automatically enrolled in the Prime option and assigned an MTF. Soldier family members choose between the two options; almost all enroll in Prime, and many are assigned to the MTF for primary care.[3] Across the MHS, 82 percent of soldier family members are enrolled in Prime. Reliance on the MTF versus civilian providers for primary care and specialty referrals depends on the strength of the network in the installation community. In metropolitan areas with Army posts such as Colorado Springs and Seattle/Tacoma, the network

---

[1] When beneficiaries enroll with primary care managers they take advantage of reduced copayments for care through the HMO-style TRICARE Prime or TRICARE Plus benefit. Non-active-duty beneficiaries may also choose not to enroll with any PCM, participate in the TRICARE Standard benefit, and make slightly larger copayments.

[2] If space is available, MTF staff will enroll beneficiaries at the MTF. Beneficiaries may request to be enrolled with civilian providers when they would otherwise have been enrolled with the MTF, but this occurs infrequently, and usually in the case where beneficiaries have specific health needs or live far from the MTF.

[3] When soldiers and dependents live distant from MTFs, they can participate in a separate program called TRICARE Prime Remote. For soldiers this should occur infrequently, such as when soldiers work as recruiters.

is very strong. In less developed areas such as Barstow, California and Fairbanks, Alaska, the network is not as well populated, and there are limited opportunities for Army beneficiaries to receive health care from places other than the MTF.

While significant attention has been given to addressing the health care needs of soldiers, especially to support their ability to deploy, Army leadership has been concerned that less attention has been paid to making sure that the health care needs of Army families are addressed throughout this cycle. There was also concern that families of soldiers who deploy may seek health care in different ways than they do when the soldier in the family is at home, e.g., by seeking care more or less frequently, or by seeking different types of care than they would under ordinary circumstances. Further, health services research has shown that stress can affect the ways in which families seek health care, and families can experience stress when soldiers deploy. Military health research has also shown instances in which family members use health care at different rates when service members deploy (Eide et al., 2010; McNulty, 2003; Gorman et al., 2010). Thus, it is important to understand family members' health care utilization throughout all phases of the deployment cycle.

Focus of This Analysis

The analysis focused on two main questions:

- How does the deployment cycle affect capacity and beneficiary utilization at Army MTFs?
- How does the deployment cycle affect family health care utilization?

To answer the first question we performed an aggregate-level analysis of installation or MTF-level effects associated with the deployment and redeployment of soldiers assigned to local units. This analysis focused on soldiers and dependent family members who relied on MTFs for their health care, at installations in the United States that deployed large numbers of soldiers, between 2004 and 2009. To answer the second question we performed a second analysis of family-level effects that analyzed the individual health care records of all Army family members between 2004 and 2009 using methods that control for all other factors and identify how their utilization differed during the period when members of the family deployed.

Aggregate-Level Analysis of Deployment Cycle Effects on Installations

The aggregate-level analysis provides a broad view of the ways in which deployment cycle events affect Army MTF capacity and utilization. For this analysis, we focused on installations in the United States that both deploy large numbers of soldiers and provide health care to Army beneficiaries. In particular, we focused on installations in the United States that deploy brigade combat teams (BCTs) and have Army hospitals. The analysis included 14 installations, which accounted for 80 percent of the soldier deployments in the time period of our analysis, 2004–2009. For each MTF, we gathered data on MTF utilization, MTF full-time equivalents (FTEs) or health care provider staffing, MTF enrollment, and personnel data for soldiers and their dependents.

We hypothesized that if large numbers of soldiers deployed concurrently, the dramatically diminished population of beneficiaries remaining near to the installations would utilize less care, in aggregate. We also expected that the total number of providers available at installations would decrease when Army units deployed, because MTFs would not bring in military, civilian, or contractor providers in sufficient quantity to offset the loss. However, we did not know which change would be larger proportionally, the decrease in providers or in beneficiaries.

We hypothesized that access to care would change when the number of providers available and the number of beneficiaries competing for appointments changed, and that families of deploying soldiers might change the way they sought care. However, we did not know whether access to care would increase or decrease, and how families would seek care differently. So we could not project what changes related to access and care-seeking behavior we would observe in utilization by the beneficiaries (dependents and nondeploying soldiers) remaining near installations when Army units deployed.

Longitudinal Analysis of Individual Family Health Care Utilization

We used regression models to estimate how families' health care utilization changed during the deployment cycle. This method compares the experience of each family when the soldier is at home to the experience of the same family when the soldier is deployed. It provides a more accurate estimate of the effects of the deployment cycle than methods that compare families of deployed soldiers to families of nondeployed soldiers.[4]

The time horizon in this analysis included the majority of the overseas contingency operations, spanning from 2004 to 2009. To address families directly affected by changes in the Army's ability to provide health care, we studied all active component family members enrolled in TRICARE Prime.

Organization of This Report

The remainder of this document is organized in three sections:

- Chapter Two describes the deployment cycle effects at installations. Specifically, this chapter explores whether deployments result in any considerable reduction in the provider capacity at MTFs and whether the MTFs retain the capacity to serve beneficiaries during deployments.
- Chapter Three describes the deployment cycle effects on individual family health care utilization.
- Chapter Four provides our conclusions and recommendations.

---

[4] To understand deployment cycle effects, we prefer the longitudinal analysis of individuals to an analysis that might compare the experience of families of deployed and nondeployed soldiers during the same period. We believe it is possible that deployment may be related to the health care utilization of a soldier's family members, i.e., a soldier with a sick family may be less likely to deploy.

CHAPTER TWO

Analysis of Deployment Cycle Effects on MTF Staffing and Aggregate Workloads

In this chapter we describe the findings from our analysis of the effects of the deployment cycle on the Army's ability to provide health care and the utilization of care by beneficiaries. We discuss the effects of the deployment cycle in the following areas: (1) beneficiary population and enrollment at the MTF, (2) health care provider availability, (3) beneficiary utilization of health care, and (4) MTF provider workload.

This chapter draws upon data from 14 installations in the United States that deploy BCTs—the fundamental unit of Army deployments—and that host Army hospitals. These installations are referred to as force platforms. As will be discussed in more detail later in this chapter, these installations account for 80 percent of deploying soldiers.

We begin the chapter with an overview of the approach used in this analysis, including a discussion of the population and data sources and of our conceptual model. Then we present the results of our analysis in the four areas listed above. We conclude with a brief summary of key points.

Overview of Approach Used in This Analysis

Population and Data Sources

For this analysis, we focused on installations in the United States that deploy BCTs and that have Army hospitals. The overlap of these conditions yielded 14 installations (Figure 2.1), which accounted for 80

Figure 2.1
U.S. Installations That Host BCTs and Army Hospitals

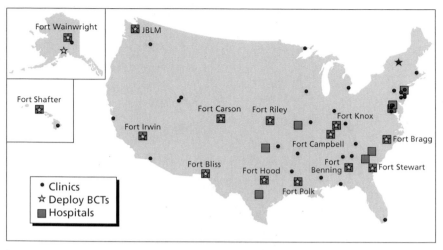

RAND *RR257-2.1*

percent of the soldier deployments in the time period of our analysis, 2004–2009. For each installation, we analyzed monthly data from the Defense Enrollment Eligibility Reporting System (DEERS) and the MHS Management Analysis and Reporting Tool (M2) health information system to understand the size of soldier and other beneficiary populations, MTF staffing, and ambulatory health care utilization. DEERS contains data for soldiers and other military beneficiaries that enable the military to provide benefits such as pay and health care. These data include residential addresses, type of TRICARE participation, and TRICARE Prime enrollment site, if relevant. For dependent beneficiaries, DEERS includes a reference to the sponsoring service member.[1] The M2 system draws MTF utilization data from the MHS electronic health record system and civilian care data from claims records filed with TRICARE. MTF provider FTE staffing by activity is recorded in the Medical Expense and Performance Reporting

---

[1] These data were crucial for our analysis of family health care utilization, as they allowed us to construct longitudinal records for spouses and children, specifying times during which the sponsoring soldier was deployed.

System (MEPRS) based on "time cards" submitted by the providers. MEPRS is one of the databases that populates M2.

We focused the analysis on the main hospital at each installation as well as any outlying outpatient clinics that are organized under the main hospital at dependent clinic locations. For the analysis, we aggregated measures of FTEs and enrollment across all locations with the same parent facility. Outlying clinics are generally located within the perimeter of the military installation, but sometimes they are located in the surrounding community to provide more convenient access to beneficiaries living off-post. Staff working at the MTF can easily be reassigned to work at either outlying clinics or the main hospital, and beneficiaries may be enrolled either to the outlying clinics or to the main hospital for primary care. When beneficiaries call to schedule an appointment, they may be given a primary care appointment at any of the clinics associated with the main MTF based on availability.

We used data from DEERS and M2 for the 14 installations. We aggregated DEERS records for all Army beneficiaries to determine, for each month:

- The number of beneficiaries with residential zip codes within a 40-mile radius of each MTF.
- The number of beneficiaries enrolled in each MTF.
- The number of soldiers enrolled at the MTF and whether they are in institutional units that do not deploy and are documented by the Army in tables of distribution and allowances (TDA) or operational units that deploy and are documented by the Army in tables of organization and equipment (TOE).
- The number of deployed and not-deployed providers. We distinguished providers assigned to operational units (TOE) and institutional units (TDA), and inferred that providers working with TDA units generally work at MTFs.[2]

---

[2]   DEERS contains data listing the Army Unit Identification Code (UIC) to which each soldier is assigned. Units can be distinguished as either TOE or TDA based on the alphanumeric properties of their UICs, but the code offers no other ways to identify any other unit characteristics useful to this analysis. Obtaining other information about a unit from UIC data requires looking up UICs individually in an Army database.

The Office of the Surgeon General provided us with an extract of M2 data measuring aggregate quantities of care delivered at the MTFs and from local civilian providers, as well as MTF provider staffing. As explained below, we used these data sources to measure the relationship between deployment cycle activities and MTFs, controlling for other factors that vary by year and installation.

Conceptual Model for Understanding How Capacity and Utilization Are Affected by the Deployment Cycle

Figure 2.2 provides an overview of the conceptual model we used to analyze the effect of deployments on health care system capacity and beneficiary health care utilization. We will first discuss the structure of the model and will then describe how we used the data sources within the model.

In this analysis, we examined the effects of soldiers' deployment in four areas:

- **Beneficiary population and enrollment at the MTF**, including soldiers, family members enrolled at the MTF, other MTF enrollees (primarily retirees and their dependents), and beneficiaries enrolled with a civilian provider.
- **Health care provider availability**, including deployment of health care providers at the same installation where soldier deployments are taking place, and provider FTEs allocated to patient care in the MTF, including active-duty, civilian, and contract providers.
- **Beneficiary utilization of care**, including utilization of outpatient care at the MTF and from civilian providers by beneficiary type and category (primary care, emergency room (ER), mental health, and surgery).
- Average MTF provider workload by category per FTE.

Our analysis quantified the following measurable parameters for each of the installations, by month:

- Soldiers enrolled at the MTF.

Figure 2.2
Conceptual Model for Understanding the Effect of Deployments on
Health Care System Capacity and Beneficiary Health Care Utilization

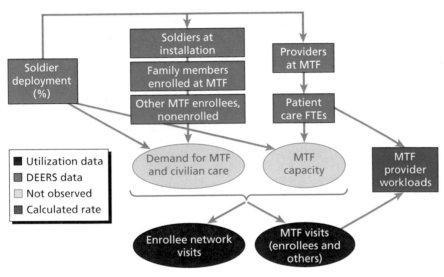

RAND *RR257-2.2*

- Portion of soldiers deployed.
- Active-duty providers enrolled at the MTF.
- Portion of active-duty providers deployed.
- Family member, retiree, and retiree dependents enrolled at the MTF.
- Provider FTEs at the MTF.
- Civilian provider visits by MTF enrollees.
- MTF visits.

Figure 2.2 shows that soldier deployment may affect the beneficiary population being served at an installation, the number of MTF providers and the FTEs devoted to patient care, and beneficiary care utilization at a given point in time (in our data, over the period of a month). Beneficiary utilization of care is the joint result of the effects of deployment on the underlying *demand* for MTF and civilian care, which is determined by the population being served (which itself may be affected by deployment), as well as MTF *capacity* to deliver care, given available staffing.

It is important to note that MTF demand and capacity are unobserved and may not be equal because there may be excess demand or excess capacity at any point in time. However, patient utilization and care provided are equal. If there is excess demand, some patients may wait longer to get care or may decide not to seek care. If there is excess capacity, patients may have easier access to care, and providers may take more time with each patient or may devote more time to other activities. If the FTE data are accurate, the changed allocation of provider time can be observed directly. We calculate the average provider workload at each MTF in each month by dividing MTF utilization (including soldiers, family members, and other beneficiaries) by the number of patient-care FTEs at the installation during the month.

The color-coding in Figure 2.2 indicates the type of data used for that component of the analysis. Purple indicates utilization data and MTF staffing data that are drawn from M2. Dark blue indicates data from DEERS that describe populations enrolled to MTFs, soldiers deployed and not deployed, and active-duty providers associated with MTFs. Green indicates rates that we calculated as a function of both utilization data and DEERS data. These rates help us understand how deployment cycle events affect the balance between the Army's ability to supply health care through the MTFs and the utilization of care by Army beneficiaries. Finally, light blue is used to indicate that we were unable to directly observe two concepts—demand for care and MTF capacity—in the data. Nonetheless, these concepts are included in the model because they drive the utilization of care that we can observe.

To estimate the relationships between soldier deployments and the four defined phenomena (beneficiary population and enrollment at the MTF, health care provider availability, beneficiary utilization of care, and average MTF provider workload), we examined data from the 14 installations in our analysis. The analysis controlled for differences across installations and other differences over time that are unrelated to the deployment cycle. Since we are using population and health care utilization data that have been aggregated at the installation level, we do not have any ability to control for demographics such as age and health status, which we know affect individuals' health care utilization.

In the following sections we will discuss the results of our analysis on the four effects listed earlier.

Effects of Soldier Deployment on Beneficiary Population and Enrollment at the MTF

We first considered the effect of deployments on Army health care beneficiary populations. For this part of the analysis, we considered both those beneficiaries who enroll at the MTFs for care and those who seek care at the MTFs without enrolling. There are three main categories of beneficiaries who receive care at MTFs: soldiers, their families, and retirees. We focus our analysis on the soldier and family member populations, as we expect these populations would be directly affected by deployment cycle events. However, we also observe any changes in retiree and retiree dependent MTF utilization to provide a control for the communities of interest. We report descriptive statistics of the beneficiary populations included in the analysis and show examples to illustrate relationships between soldier deployments and family enrollment at MTFs.

All soldiers assigned to an installation are enrolled at its MTF and seek care at the MTF unless they deploy or are referred to specialists unavailable at the MTF. In addition to enrolled soldiers, "transient" soldier populations, such as soldiers in training schools, may rely upon an MTF for care. These transient soldiers are not enrolled at the MTF (which would create an administrative burden) because they will soon be assigned to a new installation, where they can enroll for care when they arrive. Transient soldiers typically do not have a residential address filed in DEERS, so we cannot easily quantify the number of such soldiers who seek care at the MTFs in our analysis. Thus, while we included visits from nonenrolled soldiers in the total MTF workload, we did not perform an explicit analysis to understand the effects of soldier deployment on nonenrolled soldier visits, because we did not have data to track the nonenrolled population across the analysis period.

The analysis also focuses on beneficiaries other than soldiers who are reliant upon the MTFs for their health care. We characterize these populations as: soldier family members who enroll with MTFs for TRI-CARE Prime, soldier family members who live within 40 miles of the MTFs and enroll with network providers for TRICARE Prime (they are eligible to visit MTFs and do so with considerable frequency), and retirees and their dependents who enroll with MTFs through either TRICARE Prime or Plus. As noted above, we focus on soldier family members in this analysis.

We focus our analysis only on Army beneficiaries. The 14 installations in our analysis primarily serve Army beneficiaries (as opposed to other service members and eligible beneficiaries who may enroll at Army MTFs, and do so in larger numbers in multi-service communities). Of the enrolled population at these installations, 96 percent are Army beneficiaries, with only 4 percent from other services and agencies.[3]

Figure 2.3 shows the average annual enrollment for TRICARE Prime among soldiers and their family members at the 14 installations over the period of the analysis. The figure indicates that soldiers and their family members combine in almost equal proportion to make up approximately 600,000 beneficiaries enrolled at the 14 MTFs in the analysis.

The number of beneficiaries in each category increased between 2004 and 2009. The population of soldiers at the 14 installations grew from 229,000 to 314,000, an increase of 37 percent. The enrolled family member population grew as well, but at a slower rate, growing from 292,000 to 319,000 family members, an increase of 9 percent.[4] The number of family members enrolled to civilian network providers for primary care increased at a greater rate over the analysis period, growing from 49,000 to 95,000, an increase of 92 percent. By the end

---

[3] We include both TRICARE Prime and TRICARE Plus beneficiaries in this enrolled population. TRICARE Plus enrollees are beneficiaries who are over age 65 and allowed to enroll for primary care in the MTF. Their other care is generally provided in the civilian sector and financed through Medicare and the TRICARE for Life program. TRICARE Plus is available only at some MTFs and accounted for only 3 percent of enrollees in our data.

[4] The population of retirees and retiree dependents enrolled with MTFs in our analysis does not change significantly between 2004 and 2009.

Figure 2.3
Enrollment for TRICARE Prime Among Soldiers and Soldier Family Members at 14 Installations in Analysis (Average Annual Numbers)

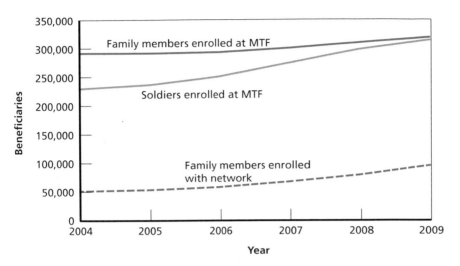

RAND *RR257-2.3*

of 2009, the number of family members in TRICARE Prime at the 14 installations was 21 percent higher than at the end of 2003. With the greatest rate of growth seen in family member populations enrolled with civilian providers, the portion of family members enrolled at the MTF decreased from 86 to 77 percent.[5]

Figure 2.4 shows increases in the soldier population enrolled at the MTF as a portion of the 2004 population for each of the 14 installations. We track soldier populations as the number of soldiers enrolled at the MTF at each installation, excluding transient soldiers such as those in training (the latter appear to be quite numerous at posts such as Fort Benning, Fort Carson, and Fort Riley). The figure indicates

---

[5] We did not investigate the reasons why the population of family members enrolled for TRICARE Prime at these installations grew at a rate slower than that of the soldier population, nor do we investigate the reasons for any of the changes in beneficiary populations over the course of the analysis. We report these data to provide background for understanding the beneficiaries reliant upon the Army for health care in order to understand their experience across deployment cycles.

Figure 2.4
Increases in Soldier Population at Forts: Annual Enrolled Soldier Population as a Portion of 2004 Population

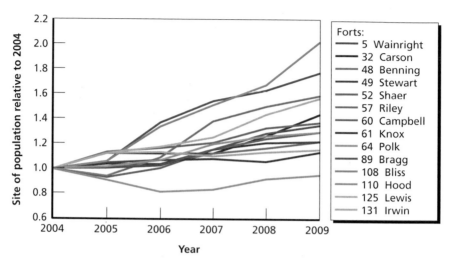

that growth in the soldier beneficiary population has not been even across installations: the legend lists the installations from greatest to least soldier population growth. Fort Bliss more than doubled the population of its enrolled soldiers, while Fort Polk experienced a decrease in its resident population of soldiers.

Since our analysis focuses on installations that host BCTs, we observe, as expected, that large portions of the soldier population at these installations deployed during our analysis period. Figure 2.5 shows the extent to which an installation's deployed population overlaps with its entire soldier population. The figure indicates that at some installations, such as Fort Stewart and Fort Campbell, as many as 80 percent of the installation's entire population was deployed at some point between 2004 and 2009,[6] while at other installations, such as

---

[6] While we could select other measures of deployment, such as average portion of soldiers deployed, we display the maximum portion of soldiers deployed. At some of the most-affected installations in the analysis the population fluctuates between mostly-at-home and

Figure 2.5
Maximum Percent of Soldiers Deployed Between 2004 and 2009

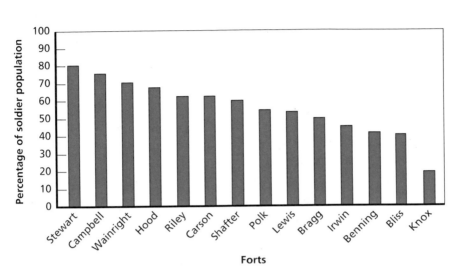

RAND *RR257-2.5*

Fort Bliss and Fort Knox (which primarily focus on missions other than deploying BCTs), a much smaller percentage of the total soldier population deployed. Although many factors influence the provision and consumption of health care at Army installations, we generally observe that installations shown toward the left of the figure (which primarily deploy units) will experience more significant deployment cycle effects, while those on the right side of the figure (which perform many missions other than deploying operational units) will experience lesser deployment cycle effects. Some very large installations located toward the center of Figure 2.5, including Fort Bragg, Fort Carson, Fort Hood, and Fort Lewis, deploy divisions while also performing other missions; these installations with very large total soldier populations are affected to a moderate degree when the divisions deploy.

The nonsoldier beneficiary population in our analysis includes soldier family members, retirees, and retiree dependents who are enrolled

---

mostly-deployed, so the average portion of soldiers deployed would represent a state that the installation experiences infrequently (see Fort Stewart population in Figure 2.6).

at the MTFs and those who are enrolled with civilian network providers for TRICARE Prime and who maintain a residential zip code within the MTF service area, which TRICARE defines as within a 40-mile radius of the MTF. Within this population, we expect that MTF enrollees are most likely to be affected by deployment because they are dependent on the MTF for their primary care and for specialty care referrals. In contrast, we expect that beneficiaries living more than 40 miles from an Army MTF do not rely on the MTF for any of their care and would not be affected by changes in MTF capacity.

We examined whether family members leave the area when soldiers deploy. Staff at Army MTFs perceived that this is common. We looked for evidence of this deployment cycle phenomenon in the family member TRICARE enrollment and residential data. In our analysis, we could not identify with statistical certainty a change in the population of soldier family members enrolled at MTFs, or residing near to MTFs, related to soldier deployments.

We show the cases of Fort Stewart and Fort Bragg, which illustrate the varying degrees with which family populations appear to change across the deployment cycle. Figures 2.6 and 2.7 show the changes in several populations across the deployment cycle. The green plot (which corresponds to the left vertical axis) represents the portion of soldiers enrolled at the MTF who are in-garrison. The blue plots (which correspond to the right axis) represent the number of family members per soldier (both soldiers in-garrison and deployed). We track changes in family members per soldier so that it is easier to identify when family members change their residential data and soldiers do not, independent of changes in the total number of soldier and family members living in the area.

Figure 2.6 shows the example case of Fort Stewart. We display the ratio of family members to soldiers so that it is easier to perceive family members who may be moving out of the area when soldiers deploy. Plotting the data in this way makes it easier to compare relative changes in the population of soldiers and family members, two populations that are of different sizes and that fluctuate in total size over the data horizon.

Figure 2.6
Fort Stewart: Percent of Soldier Population In-Garrison; Ratio of Family Members: Living in Area, Enrolled at MTF, and Enrolled with Network

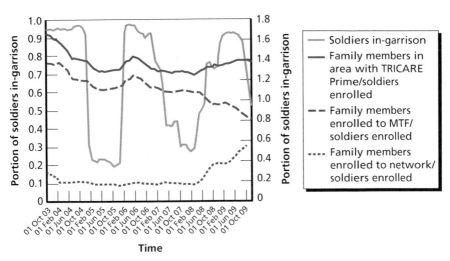

RAND *RR257 2.6*

Comparing the solid blue and green plot lines, we see a visible decrease in the ratio of family members per soldier enrolled in TRI-CARE Prime and residing in the area near the installation when the 3rd Infantry Division (ID) deploys, and a corresponding increase when the 3rd ID redeploys. This appears to support the perception of AMEDD staff that family members leave the area when soldiers deploy.

We also see a large increase in family members enrolled to the network in 2009 (relative to the soldier population), but it is not clear from these data that the increase in network enrollment is a deployment cycle event.

While the solid blue plot line represents all family members living in the MTF area and enrolled in TRICARE Prime, we used dashed and dotted blue plot lines to distinguish the segments of this population of family members that are enrolled to the MTF and to TRI-CARE network providers. We see that in 2008 the portion of TRI-CARE Prime enrolled family members enrolled to network providers increased while the population of TRICARE Prime enrolled family

Figure 2.7
Fort Bragg: Percent of Soldier Population In-Garrison; Ratio of Family Members: Living in Area, Enrolled at MTF, and Enrolled with Network

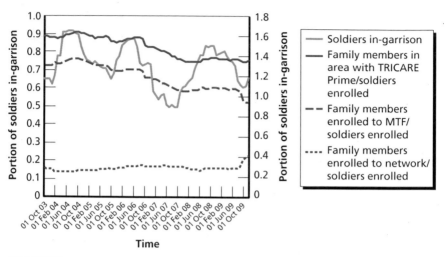

RAND RR257 2.7

members enrolled to the MTF decreased. AMEDD staff told us this change in enrollment practice was a deliberate action by Fort Stewart staff, to ease workload on the MTF. However, we have not performed analysis to fully understand the reasons for this change.

Figure 2.7 shows the example case of Fort Bragg. In this figure it is difficult to see any obvious relationship between deployment cycle events and the ratio of family members per soldier living near Fort Bragg and enrolled in TRICARE Prime.

In this section we have seen that the soldier population at the 14 installations fluctuated dramatically during the analysis period. At most installations, at least 50 percent of the total soldier population was deployed at some point. At some installations, the population of family members per soldier living in the area appeared to decrease when soldiers deployed. This may reflect family members disenrolling from the MTF and changing their residential address to one outside the geographic area when soldiers deploy. However, across the 14 locations in the analysis, we could not identify with statistical certainty a change in family member population when soldiers deploy.

Effects of Deployment on Health Care Provider Availability

We now consider the effects of deployment on the availability of health care providers. To provide context for understanding the relationship between soldier deployments and the effect on providers at the MTFs, Figure 2.8 compares the numbers of active-duty and non-active-duty providers (in terms of FTEs) over time. We include FTEs with MEPRS codes from categories A, B, E, F, G in this analysis; these categories represent the following activities, respectively: inpatient care, outpatient care, support services, special programs, and medical readiness.[7]

The figure shows a shift in the percentages of active-duty and civilian or contractor providers over time. In 2004, at the beginning of the period studied, approximately two-thirds of the FTEs at the MTFs in our analysis were active-duty, with the largest group being active-duty physicians. By the end of the analysis, in 2009, civilian and contractor providers accounted for nearly half of the FTEs at the MTFs, and the fastest-growing group consisted of civilian and contractor providers other than physicians. Four occupations—social worker, physician assistant, psychologist, and nurse practitioner—accounted for the majority of the increase in non-active-duty providers in the 14 MTFs, with the largest growth occurring in primary care and mental health.

Effect on Active-Duty Provider Deployment
We investigated the relationship between soldier deployments and active-duty provider deployments at the 14 installations. Starting in

---

[7] We included FTEs and MEPRS codes contributed by providers who typically provide patient care. We included both type 1 and type 2 providers, who in the MHS are defined as clinicians and direct care professionals. These definitions serve to distinguish physicians and nonphysicians. We excluded MEPRS codes C and D, which refer to dental care and ancillary services, as we assumed the providers who generate FTEs for these activities do not typically provide patient care (other than dental).

Figure 2.8
FTEs at 14 MTFs in Analysis

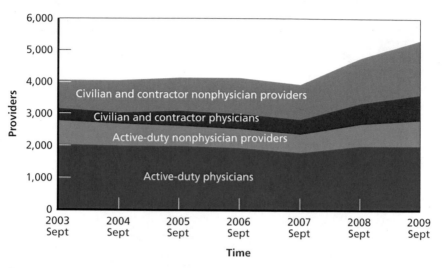

RAND *RR257-2.8*

2005, the Army Medical Department (AMEDD) regularly held a Professional Filler System (PROFIS) Deployment Conference[8] to allocate provider deployment requirements to its MTFs, allowing the deployment burden for active-duty providers to be spread across AMEDD facilities, and reducing the effect of soldier deployments on the MTFs at the local installation. As a result, we expected that the relationship between soldiers deploying with operational units and active-duty providers deploying from the same installation might be moderate. After the establishment of the PROFIS system, providers who deployed with operational units could be sourced from installations other than the same fort as the operational units.[9] To understand the effects of an

---

[8] *FRAGMENTARY ORDER (FRAGO) 12 TO MEDCOM Operation Order 04-01,* 14 March 2005. This order established the sourcing system by which active-duty medical staff are drawn from units other than the local MTF when operational units gain medical staff while preparing to deploy.

[9] Providers fill deploying positions in a number of operational units, including medical units such as combat support hospitals and combat units such as BCTs. Whether medical

installation's soldier deployments on the deployment of health care providers at the same installation, we performed a regression analysis across the 14 locations in our analysis, using a specification that controls for differences between installations and other differences over time that are unrelated to the deployment cycle.

To characterize the population of providers assigned to operational units compared to those assigned to MTFs, we distinguished between active-duty providers assigned to TOE units and those assigned to TDA units. By definition, providers assigned to TOE units are part of the deploying population, while providers assigned to TDA units are generally working at MTFs.[10,11]

There is a strong relationship between the deployment of soldiers from an installation and the deployment of TOE providers—those assigned to operational units. There is a much weaker relationship between soldier deployment and the deployment of providers assigned to TDA units (the MTFs). Across the 14 installations, our statistical analysis shows that the relationship between total soldier deployments and TOE provider deployments is 0.81. In contrast, the relationship between total soldier deployments and TDA provider deployments is only 0.04.[12]

---

units and combat units from the same installation deploy simultaneously may contribute to the relationship between soldier deployments and provider deployments. As with PROFIS, we did not measure the extent to which these policies caused the relationship between soldier and provider deployments.

[10] We slightly overestimate the number of providers assigned to MTFs by defining all providers assigned to TDA units as working at MTFs. In reality, there may be a small number of providers working in institutional units that are not MTFs; however, this number should be very small.

[11] When we estimated the regression to measure the relationship between total soldier deployments and active-duty provider deployments, we included providers in the total soldier population. So there is inherently a small degree of correlation in the total population of soldiers and the population of providers. However, the number of active-duty providers is so small relative to the total soldier population that we believe the results from the regression analysis will be dominated by the relationship we aim to address, the coincidence of operational unit deployment and active-duty provider deployment, rather than the overlap of the populations.

[12] Results are significant at the 0.05 level.

The results of the analysis are shown in Figure 2.9, plotted as an example. Consider an installation the size of Fort Stewart, which is a mid-size deployment platform. Across the analysis horizon, Fort Stewart had on average 20,226 soldiers, 146 TOE health care providers assigned to operational units, and 234 TDA health care providers. For this example, we will consider a representative soldier deployment of 40 percent. The results indicate that when 40 percent of soldiers deploy, 32 percent of the providers assigned to TOE units, and 2 percent of the providers assigned to the TDA units (the MTF), would likely deploy.

We can also look at the relationship between soldier deployments and health care provider deployments for a specific location and point in time. While we used the demographics at Fort Stewart as a basis to provide an example of the average aggregate relationship between soldier and provider deployments, the specific experience at Fort Stewart, and of all the other installations in the analysis, varied from the aggregate result. There are instances, during some time periods and at some installations, in which the relationship is stronger or weaker.

Figure 2.9
Correlation of Provider-to-Soldier Deployments

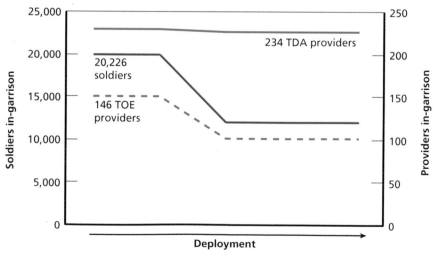

We provide examples of individual installations in Figures 2.10 and 2.11. Figure 2.10 shows the example of Fort Stewart, which houses Winn Army Community Hospital and is one of the "purest" deployment platforms in the analysis. We showed earlier that Fort Stewart achieves a nearly 80 percent concurrent deployment of soldiers and providers from the post, the highest deployment rate out of the 14 posts we studied. At Fort Stewart there is a very strong relationship between the rate of deployment of soldiers and TOE providers, while there is a weaker, yet visible, relationship between the deployment of soldiers and MTF providers. During 2005, when the 3rd ID deployed from Fort Stewart, almost 20 percent of TDA providers deployed. When the 3rd ID deployed in 2007–2008, about 15 percent of TDA providers deployed. Across the years studied, the baseline TDA provider deployment rate at Fort Stewart was approximately 10 percent, so the increase in TDA provider deployment occurring with the two 3rd ID deployments was roughly 5 to 10 percent.

Figure 2.10
Soldiers and Active-Duty Providers, Percentage In-Garrison,
Fort Stewart—3rd ID

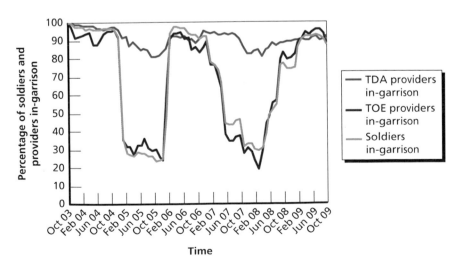

Figure 2.11
Soldiers and Active-Duty Providers, Percentage In-Garrison,
Fort Bragg—82nd Airborne

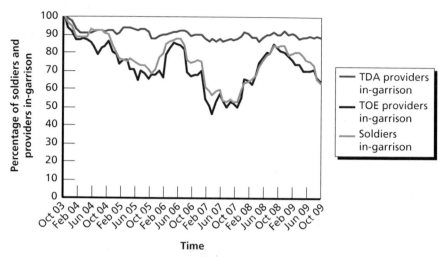

When we look at similar data from Fort Bragg (Figure 2.11), we see a weaker relationship between soldier and provider deployments. Fort Bragg, compared to Fort Stewart and many of the other installations in our analysis, is a very large installation that performs missions other than deploying the 82nd Airborne Division. Its total soldier population is around 82,000, while the total soldier population at Fort Stewart is around 43,000. Womack Army Medical Center at Fort Bragg operates a number of graduate medical education programs, and providers assigned to the education programs may be exempted from deployment responsibilities. There are around 780 active-duty providers working at Fort Bragg, compared to only 230 active-duty providers working at Winn Army Community Hospital at Fort Stewart.

At Fort Bragg we see a strong relationship between soldiers deploying and TOE providers deploying, but the rate of TDA provider deployment is generally consistent across our analysis horizon from 2004 to 2009. There was little or no visible surge in TDA provider deployment when the 82nd Airborne Division deployed in 2005 and 2007. The weaker relationship is likely attributable to the large population of 780 active-duty providers working at the installation, who do not deploy or whose deployments are not synchronized with the division.

Effect on FTEs, MTF Provider Time Allocated to Patient Care

Having observed the relationship between soldier deployments and active-duty provider deployments, we next consider how soldier deployments affect the FTEs recorded at installation MTFs for patient care and other activities.

MTFs have options for managing health care providers across the deployment cycle. They may hire more civilian or contractor providers when active-duty providers deploy. Alternatively, they may reallocate the type of work that active-duty providers perform at different points in the deployment cycle, e.g., directing providers to perform nonpatient care activities such as military training and continuing professional education during periods when they are in less demand at the MTF.

Using the same regression analysis method described earlier, we estimated the relationship between soldier deployments and FTEs recorded at installation MTFs. We counted FTEs for both physician and nonphysician providers, including active-duty, contractor, and civilian. The results, shown in Figure 2.12, indicate that when soldiers deploy, there is a slight, and statistically insignificant, decrease in the total number of FTEs recorded at installation MTFs, consistent with the small estimated increase in MTF provider deployments. The results suggest that the decrease will be largely composed of outpatient-care FTEs, which are B-type MEPRS codes in the MTF manpower accounting system. There may also be a decrease in outpatient-care FTEs of 5 percent. Of the results shown in Figure 2.12, only those for outpatient care FTEs are statistically significant at the conventional 0.05 level.

In summary, when soldiers deploy, the providers assigned to operational units tend also to deploy, while only a smaller percentage of providers assigned to MTFs deploy, and the relationship between soldier deployments and MTF provider deployments varied by installation. We observed little change across the deployment cycle in total provider FTEs at the MTFs, although we observed a slight decrease in outpatient-care FTEs when soldiers deployed.

Figure 2.12
Relationship Between 40 Percent Soldier Deployment and Provider FTEs,
Results Across All Installations in Analysis

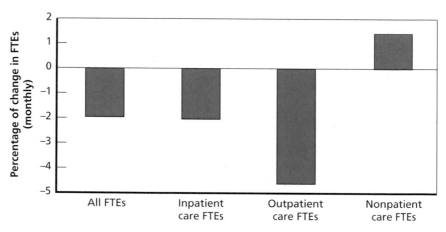

NOTE: All results significant at the 0.05 level.
RAND RR257-2.12

Effects of Deployment on Outpatient Utilization

As we discussed earlier, utilization of MTF and network health care is related to both beneficiary demand for health care services, and MTF and other provider capacity to provide services. Earlier in this chapter we showed the relationship between soldier deployment and a substantial decrease in the soldier population at the installation, with some possible relocation of deploying soldiers' family members, but overall little change in the family member, retiree, and retiree dependent population in the area or their enrollment at the MTF. However, the degree of population change appears to vary considerably across installations.[13] The impact of deployment on MTF staffing is very small overall, although it may be significant at times for individual clinical services. These results suggest that, overall, MTF utilization *by soldiers*

---

[13] The change at Fort Stewart (Figure 2.6) appears to be among the most distinct examples of family members leaving the area when soldiers deploy.

should be noticeably affected by deployment, but that we would expect to see little effect on MTF utilization *by other beneficiaries.*

Background: Patterns of Health Care Utilization by Beneficiary Group

To provide the basis for understanding deployment effects on overall MTF utilization, we first provide an overview of utilization by beneficiary groups. As shown in Figure 2.13, the share of MTF visits generated by different beneficiary groups varies. In Figure 2.3, we saw that soldiers and their family members accounted for approximately the same portion of the population enrolled at the MTF in 2009. Including enrolled retiree and retiree dependents, soldiers and family members accounted for 44 and 41 percent of enrolled beneficiaries, respectively, in October 2009. However, despite relatively similar enrollment percentages, soldiers utilize MTF care at approximately twice the rate of family members. As a result, soldiers accounted for 57 percent of MTF visits, whereas family members accounted for only 26 percent of MTF visits (Figure 2.13). Soldiers generate the highest number of visits

Figure 2.13
Portion of MTF Visits at 14 Installations, by Beneficiary Group, October 2009

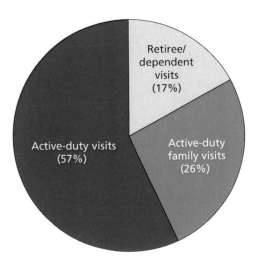

per enrollee, while family members generate the lowest number of visits per enrollee, and retirees and their dependents generate visits at a per-enrollee rate between those of soldiers and family members.

Although soldiers use more care overall than family members, they use less civilian care. Figure 2.14 compares the average number of MTF and civilian network visits for soldiers and family members enrolled to the 14 MTFs in our analysis, using averages during 2004 and 2009. These data also include the population of family members enrolled with civilian network providers for primary care in the communities surrounding the MTFs.[14] We do not include in our analysis the population of soldiers (fewer than 1 percent) who enroll with network providers for primary care. We performed this comparison using Relative Value Units (RVUs) rather than visits to better compare care at MTFs and care at civilian network providers. RVUs are a measure of productivity used to compare the resources required to perform patient care services. RVUs capture differences in the types of care being provided in the two settings.[15]

In Figure 2.14 we show average utilization rates from years 2004 and 2009. We see that soldiers have substantially more frequent visits overall, and almost all of their visits are to the MTFs. Family members who are enrolled at the MTFs visit the MTF less frequently than soldiers and have only slightly more utilization of civilian providers. In comparison, family members enrolled to civilian network providers have the lowest overall visit rate and, as we would expect, the highest rate of civilian visits.

---

[14] We identify family members enrolled in civilian networks as those who both have zip codes within a 40-mile radius of the MTF and are enrolled with TRICARE Prime with a civilian network provider. We believe that the zip code data for families in our analysis are as accurate as the data for TRICARE enrollment, as both data are required for beneficiaries to be eligible for health care. When we compared changes in populations enrolled to MTFs and those living near to MTFs, we saw that these populations increased and decreased in unison. However, it is possible that family members do not update this data promptly when they move.

[15] In other analysis of MTF utilization, we observed nearly identical trends when studying RVUs and visits, leading us to believe that the relationship between RVUs and visits recorded at MTFs should not change over the deployment cycle.

Figure 2.14
Rate of Health Care Utilization by Soldier and Family Members at 14
Installations, Averages in 2004 and 2009

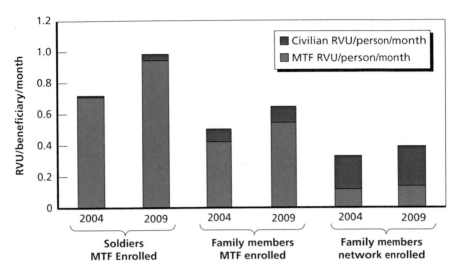

RAND RR257-2.14

We were not surprised to find that soldiers utilize care at a greater rate than family members. In order to be excused from work or get a reprieve from physical training, soldiers[16] are required to get a temporary profile—a doctor's note—that describes their medical condition and exemption. Soldiers must visit a provider to receive permission to be excused from duty and are not allowed to self-prescribe bed-rest for minor conditions, as civilians are. When soldiers attend sick call at a Troop Medical Clinic or an outpatient clinic at an Army hospital, these visits are recorded as utilization in the electronic medical record

---

[16] Adherence to this requirement is not uniform. In practice soldiers may adhere to this requirement to the extent mandated by their leadership. We would expect that this policy is applied more strictly to junior enlisted soldiers than to higher-ranking noncommissioned officers and officers.

and appear in the data we gathered for our analysis.[17] We expect that the need for soldiers to attend sick call to be relieved from duty is one major reason that soldiers appear to use care at a much greater rate than their family members. In addition, the requirement for soldiers to remain medically ready generates additional visits to establish more-permanent soldier medical profiles and to help soldiers work through their medical conditions.

We also note that family members who are enrolled to civilian providers utilize care at a rate that is 40 percent lower than family members enrolled to MTFs. These two populations may not be equivalent: family members' decisions to enroll with MTFs or civilian network providers may be related to their health care needs and the way they prefer to seek health care. Once enrolled, there may be differences in access mechanisms (such as methods to make appointments and appointment availability) in the two sectors. It is also possible that using RVUs to measure utilization does not fully capture differences in the type or purpose of the visits made to MTF versus civilian providers. Finally, MTF and civilian providers may differ in their return-visit and referral rates. We did not perform any analysis to compare whether these populations were similar demographically; it was beyond the scope of this analysis to explore the contributions of these potential explanations for utilization differences.

Effects on Outpatient Utilization

We next consider how utilization of care changes at MTFs across the deployment cycle, first looking at utilization by soldiers and then by family members and retirees and their dependents. Prior to deployment and when redeploying (returning home), soldiers are required to visit a primary care provider for a health screening and to complete a health questionnaire. Mental and physical health conditions are assessed during these deployment health screenings, and referrals for additional care are initiated as required.

---

[17] Our data appear to capture little of the care received outside these clinics from providers assigned to soldiers' units during this time period.

MTF Utilization

Relatively higher rates of soldier utilization may be due in part to required health assessments that soldiers must complete periodically. Soldiers must complete a Periodic Health Assessment (PHA) every year in order to remain eligible to deploy. Soldiers may complete these assessments well in advance of a deployment, but some may hurry to complete them in the months preceding their scheduled deployment. This can lead to a surge in demand for appointments by soldiers at the MTF, especially when soldiers deploy in large numbers, such as when a BCT with more than 2,500 soldiers, or a division with three or four BCTs, deploys.

When soldiers redeploy, they must complete a Post-Deployment Health Assessment (PDHA) within 30 days of their return. In the course of completing these assessments, soldiers may be referred to specialists to address injuries that occurred during deployment. Each of these referrals is managed under a standard of "heightened access to care" and must occur within seven days of the referral.

Recently, Post-Deployment Health Re-Assessments (PDHRAs) have been mandated for soldiers 90 days after they redeploy. When large numbers of soldiers schedule these exams simultaneously, this may also cause a surge in demand for appointments at the MTF. When soldiers redeploy in large numbers, these referrals may place a burden on MTF specialty clinics, and may restrict access for other beneficiaries.

Our analysis was designed to determine whether the amount of care sought by soldiers and other beneficiary groups changes in relation to deployment cycle events. As with PHAs, the simultaneous demand for PDHA exams after a large-scale redeployment may cause a surge for demand at the MTF. We examined several types of care (primary care, surgery, ER, orthopedics, mental health). Primary care constituted 53 percent of outpatient visits for retirees and their dependents, and 57 percent of outpatient visits for soldier family members. Figure 2.15 shows the relationship between soldier deployment and utilization of several types of care by soldiers, and utilization of primary care

Figure 2.15
Change in Monthly Outpatient and Primary Care Visits Per Enrolled Beneficiary When 40 Percent of Soldiers Deploy

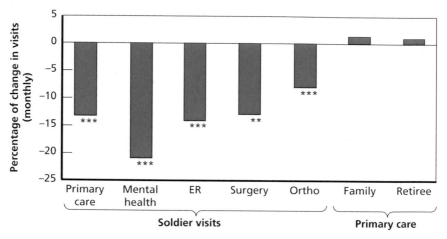

** Results significant at the 0.05 level.
*** Results significant at the 0.01 level.

RAND RR257-2.15

by other beneficiaries.[18] For all the following results, we performed a regression analysis, controlling for trends in time and variances across installations.

We found that when soldiers deploy, the rate of MTF visits per enrolled soldier decreases, although at a rate less than the decrease in soldier population in-garrison at the installation (Figure 2.15). We interpret this result to mean that the decrease in the soldier population in-garrison has a large effect on soldier visits to the MTF, but that there are other factors that influence the number of soldier visits to the MTF and account for higher rates of visits by those soldiers who do not deploy.

In contrast, we observed a weak relationship between soldier deployments and utilization by the other beneficiary categories (family members, retirees, and their dependents). We noted a slight increase

---

[18] Changes in family member, retiree, and retiree dependent utilization of other types of care followed similar patterns as changes in primary care utilization.

in the rate of per-enrollee utilization by these beneficiary groups when soldiers deployed, but the magnitude of the increase is very small and not statistically significant. In the next section we show that, on an individual level, the families of deployed soldiers experience a somewhat larger decrease in MTF utilization. But overall, deployment has had little impact on aggregate MTF utilization for family members, retirees, and their dependents at these 14 major installations.

We provide a view of the relationship between soldier deployments and soldier visits at the installation level, in this case for Fort Stewart (Figure 2.16) and Fort Bragg (Figure 2.17). In both cases we see that the number of soldier visits to the MTF increases and decreases with the soldier population in-garrison. However, in both cases, the peaks and valleys of soldier visits to the MTF are smaller than the peaks and valleys of the changes in soldier population in-garrison. This phenomenon is most clear for Fort Stewart. In the time period surrounding the deployment of the 3rd ID in 2005, the soldier population decreased from 40,000 to 10,000, and subsequently increased again to 40,000 when the soldiers redeployed. But the figure shows a smaller relative

Figure 2.16
Fort Stewart Soldier Population In-Garrison and Soldier MTF Visits

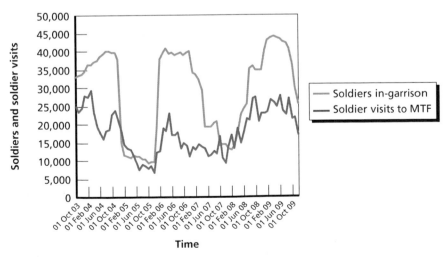

Figure 2.17
Fort Bragg Soldier Population In-Garrison and Soldier MTF Visits

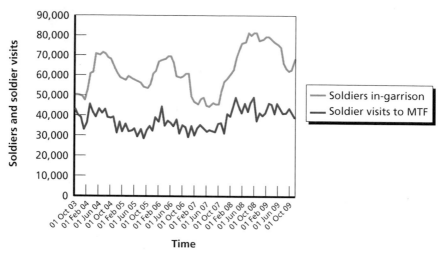

decrease in the quantity of soldier visits to the MTF. In this same time period, we see a decrease from 20,000 visits to 10,000 visits at the time of deployment, and an increase to 20,000 visits again at the time of redeployment. In this example, the relative decrease in the number of soldier visits is not as large as the relative decrease in the number of soldiers in-garrison. We also observe that the number of soldier MTF visits per soldier in-garrison changes across the deployment cycle. We will discuss this phenomenon further below.

In Figure 2.16, we showed that the rate of MTF visits per enrolled soldier decreases at the MTFs in our analysis when soldiers deploy, but only by a fraction of the departing beneficiaries. We now explore reasons for this occurrence, including the role of several contributing factors:

1. Visits by nonenrolled soldiers are included in the rates displayed in Figures 2.16–2.17, but we lack data to include these transient soldiers in our population counts.

2. Soldiers who do not deploy may seek care differently than those who do, as nondeploying soldiers may be restricted from deploying for medical reasons.
3. When a large number of soldiers are deployed, access to care may change for those beneficiaries who do not deploy.

We will examine the relationship between soldier deployments and soldier MTF visits further to evaluate the extent to which these phenomena may contribute to deployment cycle effects at Army installations.

Effect of Nonenrolled Soldiers on Number of MTF Visits

We need to be aware that nonenrolled soldiers may constitute a sizable portion of MTF visits. Since we do not have data to describe the population of nonenrolled soldiers in this analysis, we make a simple assumption that the number of MTF visits from this group neither increases nor decreases in relation to the deployment cycle.[19] In Figure 2.18 we see that enrolled soldiers account for approximately 75 percent of the visits to MTFs at most of the installations in our analysis.

With the same example of a 40 percent soldier deployment and the aggregate soldier population, we expect an overall decrease in soldier MTF visits of only 28 percent. This expected result accounts for the muting effect of nonenrolled soldier visits on the visit total, assuming no relationship between deployments and visits by nonenrolled soldiers.

Utilization Patterns Among Nondeployed Soldiers and Access to Care for Beneficiaries

We studied the relationship between soldier deployment and the rate at which TOE and TDA soldier populations utilize care at MTFs. We used the same soldier deployment data to represent deployment cycle effects as we have in all the analyses. We observed how the monthly

---

[19] Assuming no relationship between nonenrolled soldier visits and deployments may underestimate the extent to which nonenrolled soldier visits mute deployment cycle effects. We expect that MTF staff could manage visits by nonenrolled soldiers to move preventive or mandatory readiness visits to times when the deployment cycle is lower. To support management decisions at MTFs, we recommend using information about nonenrolled soldier visits to manage MTF resources. But underestimating this effect will not have biased the empirical results we observe for changes in visits by enrolled nondeploying soldiers.

Figure 2.18
Percentage of Soldier Visits to MTF by Soldiers Enrolled at the Installation,
Average over 2004–2009

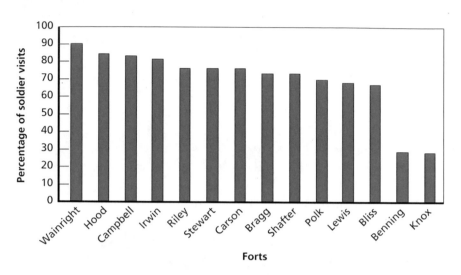

RAND RR257-2.18

rate of TDA and TOE soldier visits per enrolled TDA and TOE soldier changed. We also restricted the population to TDA and TOE soldiers who are in-garrison during the month of observation, excluding from the population soldiers who are deployed during part of the month, and the visits generated by those soldiers.

In Figure 2.19 we see the changes in rate of visits per nondeploying TOE and TDA soldiers, observing first the TDA soldiers, since very few TDA soldiers deploy. If 40 percent of the total number of soldiers assigned to a fort in this analysis deploy, on average 93 percent of TDA soldiers would remain in-garrison. During deployments there is little change in the in-garrison population of TDA soldiers. But their visit rates increase by 8 percent when 40 percent of soldiers deploy. Thus, it appears that TDA soldiers have easier access to care during a deployment.

When we look at the population of TOE soldiers, we see greater changes in population during deployments. When 40 percent of the soldiers from an installation deploy, nearly all of the deploying soldiers

Figure 2.19
**Change in Monthly Rate of Local MTF Visits by TOE and TDA Enrolled
Soldiers When 40 Percent of Soldiers Deploy**

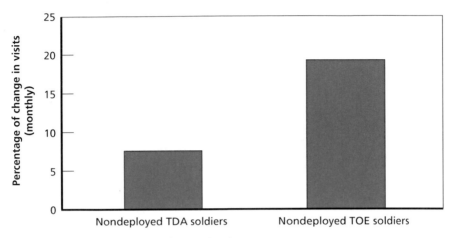

NOTE: All results significant at the 0.01 level.
RAND RR257-2.19

will come from TOE units, and on average only 54 percent of the
TOE soldiers would remain in-garrison. While the TDA population
in-garrison changes little when soldiers deploy, nearly all of the deploying soldiers will come from the TOE population. This population *does*
change during deployments. And when 40 percent of soldiers deploy,
the increase in rate of visits is higher for the TOE population than the
TDA population. The rate of TOE soldier visits increases 19 percent,
when 40 percent of soldiers deploy.

We saw that installation factors such as an increase in access to
care, independent of sizable changes in population, were associated
with an 8 percent increase in the rate of TDA soldier utilization. When
we turned to the TOE population, which experiences a far greater
decrease during deployments, we observed a greater increase in soldier
visits, by 19 percent.

In addition to experiencing similar installation effects—such as
access to care changes—as the TDA population, TOE soldiers who
remain in-garrison may have different health care needs than those
who deploy. Among many possible reasons for this difference, the non-

deploying TOE soldiers may have medical reasons for remaining in-garrison and may visit the MTF more frequently to meet their medi-cal needs and become medically deployable. The results in Figure 2.19 thus show the combined effect of changes in access and population.

Civilian Network Provider Utilization

We also consider whether outpatient care by Army soldiers and family members changes at civilian providers across the deployment cycle. In Figure 2.14 we showed that soldiers enrolled to MTFs utilize a mini-mal amount of outpatient care from civilian providers, 4 percent of their utilization.[20] Family members enrolled to MTFs use slightly more care from civilian providers, 16 percent of their utilization. Not sur-prisingly, family members enrolled to civilian providers for primary care receive most of their care from civilian providers, 63 percent of their utilization.

Looking across these populations, we see a 27 percent decrease in the rate of civilian care utilization by soldiers (Figure 2.20). However, we recall that soldiers in this analysis do not utilize much care from civilian providers, so this large relative decrease is not a large change in absolute quantity of utilization. We see a very slight increase in out-patient utilization from civilian providers by families enrolled to the MTF, and a small decrease by families enrolled to the civilian provider network. Looking across the entire population of family members enrolled for TRICARE Prime near the installations in our analysis, we observe little aggregate change in outpatient utilization from civil-ian providers across the deployment cycle. In the next chapter we will discuss in greater detail the ways in which outpatient care utilization by family members changes when soldiers deploy.

In sum, we have seen in this section that soldier utilization at the MTFs decreased significantly when soldiers deploy, but at a lower rate than the decrease in enrolled soldiers in-garrison. Nondeploying soldiers used more care when soldiers deployed, while visits by family

---

[20] This portion is measured by comparing beneficiary-generated RVUs from MTFs and civilian providers. When we presented this data initially, we noted that there are reasons why RVUs from MTFs and RVUs from civilian providers may not represent care that beneficia-ries utilize in precisely the same way.

Figure 2.20
Change in Monthly Rate of Civilian Provider RVUs by Soldiers and Family Members When 40 Percent of Soldiers Deploy

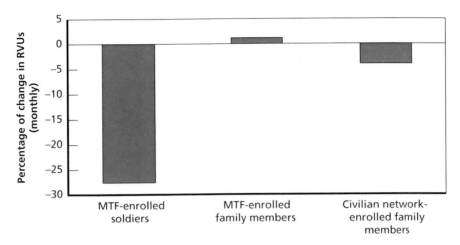

NOTE: All results significant at the 0.01 level.

RAND RR257-2.20

members, retirees, and their dependents did not change significantly across the deployment cycle. There was also little change in family member visits to civilian providers when soldiers deployed.

Effects of Deployment on MTF Provider Workload

We now consider the effects of deployment on MTF provider workload. We are interested in whether providers at the MTFs appear to be overly taxed when soldiers deploy. Although we posit in our conceptual model (Figure 2.2) that deployment will decrease patient-care FTEs, those FTEs actually decrease only slightly when soldiers deploy (Figure 2.12), in rough proportion to the TDA providers who deploy from the installation. However, visits to the MTF do not change significantly for family members, retirees, and retiree dependents when soldiers deploy, and soldier visits decrease (Figure 2.15).

If there is little change in patient-care FTEs at the MTFs, and a decrease in visits, then we would expect to see provider workloads decrease when soldiers deploy. Using the regression model, we saw that across all types of care, the number of outpatient MTF visits per provider outpatient FTE decreases by about 6 percent when 40 percent of the soldiers deploy.[21]

Chapter Summary

We recap the findings in this section of the report by turning again to the conceptual model to put the findings in perspective. In Figure 2.21 we reproduce the conceptual model with notes in red font to suggest the effects observed.

Starting at the upper left corner of the figure, we show the range of peak simultaneous deployment (also shown in Figure 2.5), which is roughly 40 to 80 percent, and we select a representative example of 40 percent deployment to explain deployment cycle effects. Figures 2.6 and 2.7 showed that although deployment cycle changes in family enrollment were difficult to detect, it appeared that in some cases as many as 45 percent of families of deploying soldiers may leave the area during deployment. Figure 2.9 illustrated that, when 40 percent of soldiers deployed, 32 percent of TOE providers and 2 percent of TDA providers deployed. These provider deployments appeared to have little effect on patient-care FTEs, which decreased by only 5 percent when 40 percent of soldiers were deployed (Figure 2.12). Despite all these changes to the inputs that affect demand for care and MTF capacity, we observed little change in civilian care visits by TRICARE Prime enrollees, and little change in visits to the MTF by family members, retirees, and retiree beneficiaries. Soldiers enrolled to MTFs use little civilian care in total (Figure 2.14). However, we saw that MTF visits decreased by 13 percent when 40 percent of the soldiers deployed from an installation. During the same time periods, visits by nondeployed

---

[21] Results significant at the 0.01 level.

Figure 2.21
Deployment Cycle Effects: Populations and Soldier MTF Visits

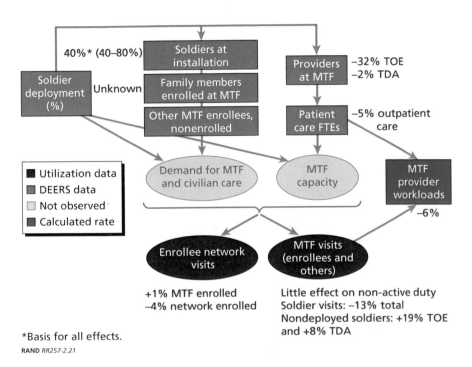

*Basis for all effects.
RAND RR257-2.21

TDA soldiers increased by 8 percent, and visits by nondeployed TOE soldiers increased by 19 percent (Figure 2.19).

In this chapter we answered the question, How does the deployment cycle affect capacity and beneficiary utilization at Army MTFs? We observed the following effects.

Beneficiary Population and Enrollment

The soldier population in-garrison at the 14 installations fluctuated dramatically across the analysis horizon, with most installations experiencing more than 50 percent of the soldiers deploying concurrently. In some cases, families appeared to leave the area when soldiers deployed, but it is difficult to discern precisely the deployment cycle effect.

Health Care Provider Availability

When soldiers deployed, most of the providers assigned to operational units also deployed. We observed only a small correlation between soldier deployments and deployments of providers assigned to MTFs. However, the effect seen within different installations varied.

We observed little change across the deployment cycle in total provider FTEs at the MTFs, including active-duty, civilian, and contract providers. When soldiers deployed, we observed a slight decrease in outpatient-care FTEs.

Outpatient Utilization

Soldier utilization at the MTF decreased significantly when soldiers deployed, but decreased in only one-third proportion to the decrease in enrolled soldiers in-garrison. Nondeploying soldiers used more care when soldiers deployed. In aggregate, family member visits and visits by retirees and their dependents did not change significantly across the deployment cycle.

Soldiers make very few visits to civilian providers, but we observed a decrease in soldier visits to civilian providers when soldiers deployed. There was little change in aggregate family member visits to civilian providers when soldiers deployed.

Provider Workload

There was little change across the deployment cycle in provider FTEs available for outpatient care at the MTFs and a significant decrease in soldier visits. Thus, we see a corresponding decrease in the outpatient workload per provider FTE when soldiers deploy.

Army's Overall Ability to Provide Care

At the outset of the analysis we asked whether the Army's ability to provide care at its MTFs was in balance with beneficiary utilization across the deployment cycle. Since the aggregate workload per provider FTE at the MTFs decreases when soldiers deploy, and aggregate utilization by family members and retirees and their dependents does not change significantly, we conclude that access to care by family members does not appear impinged, in the aggregate. Even so, we note from related research that the ability to provide specialized care may be impinged by the deployment cycle (Sorbero et al., 2013).

CHAPTER THREE

How Does Family Health Care Utilization Change in Response to the Deployment Cycle?

We now summarize the ways in which deployment cycle events affect individual family member health care utilization. The VCSA, sponsor of this project, expressed concern that families' health care needs may change in relation to the deployment cycle, and that these needs may not be fully addressed by Army policies. Based on prior research, we have further reason for concern that deployments may have adverse effects on the well-being of Army families, thus increasing their need for care. Mansfield et al. (2010) document higher rates of depressive, sleep, and anxiety disorders among the wives of deployed versus non-deployed soldiers, and Chandra et al. (2010a), Flake et al. (2009), and Chartrand et al. (2008) identified strong negative associations between parental deployments and a range of child difficulties such as psychosocial functioning and behavior problems.

The analysis we report in this chapter made unique contributions in examining how deployment cycle events affect the experience of soldiers and family members. We studied the relationship between deployment cycle events and family members' utilization of direct care (from MTFs) and civilian network care (from civilian network providers.) We also included ER utilization and pharmaceutical utilization in our analysis. The scope and method used are broader than found in prior studies. While other studies of families and service member deployment have focused on specific time periods or populations (Doperak, 2009, and Mansfield et al., 2011), we include the majority of the overseas contingency operations from 2004 to 2009 in our analysis, and all active component family members who were enrolled in TRICARE Prime. Further, while previous studies have generally focused on a specific time period and compared the experience of families who had a soldier deployed to that of families who did not, we assess the experiences of families longitudinally over six years, comparing the experience of families when a soldier is at home to the experience of the same family when the soldier is deployed.[1] This methodology allowed us to control better for the uniqueness of each family's health care experience, and to understand more completely the effect of deployment cycle events on families' health care utilization. We will describe the experience of spouses and children with general outpatient care and ER care, as well as specific analyses of mental health care utilization and pharmaceutical utilization.

Data Sources

To conduct this analysis, we employed individual level data from the DEERS and the M2. We assembled a longitudinal record of outpatient care for each Army family member. We included the limited demographic data available for family members (e.g., age, gender, ethnicity). We linked the family members to the sponsoring soldiers with unique data identifiers created by the Defense Manpower Data Center (DMDC), which allowed us also to identify all the health care records and the sponsoring soldier for an individual family member without identifying the member or soldier. We included outpatient care from the MTF and civilian providers for all family members, including those enrolled in TRICARE Prime as well as TRICARE Standard and Extra.

We studied outpatient care from the Standard Ambulatory Data Record (SADR) and TRICARE Encounters Data Non-Institutional

---

[1] In order to perform the longitudinal analysis, we restricted the analysis to active component soldiers and family members. Beneficiaries from the reserve components do not use TRICARE outside of time periods immediately preceding, during, and immediately following soldier deployments. So we cannot longitudinally account for their full health care utilization through TRICARE data, as we can for beneficiaries in the active component.

(TEDNI). We excluded the small amount of outpatient care delivered by civilian network providers that is delivered at institutional facilities run by hospitals, in order to perform the analysis without processing claims from TRICARE Encounters Data Institutional (TEDI). We never possessed identified data over the course of this analysis.

We captured the experience of 339,000 spouses and 537,000 children of active component soldiers. We gathered health care utilization data for the entire population of TRICARE Prime enrolled soldier family members between 2004 and 2009. Most spouses and children lived in the same zip code as the soldier, 81 percent and 79 percent respectively. When we address deployment cycle effects on children of single parents, these are the minority, approximately 15 percent of children. Of these children of single parents, approximately three-quarters had the same residential zip code as the soldier. Aided by the large sample size, we can report that all results in this section are statistically significant.

We used regression models to separate deployment cycle effects from other trends in beneficiary health care utilization, and to control for differences among families.

We also assessed whether a soldier's or soldier's family's health status affected his propensity to deploy, but we did not observe a significant relationship and thus do not present these results.

Changes in Spouse Health Care Utilization

We begin this analysis by looking longitudinally at health care utilization by spouses of soldiers and compare the utilization within a single family during deployment and nondeployment periods. To assess episodes of care, we observed health care utilization, for each beneficiary in the analysis, monthly through the analysis period, noting in which months a soldier in the family was deployed. We analyzed the likelihood that a beneficiary would utilize care in a given month, measuring both the likelihood that beneficiaries used any type of care, and also specifying a few care types of particular interest, such as emergency room and mental health.

We counted all MTF visits recorded in SADR, and all civilian network provider visits with claims recorded in TEDNI. We sought to analyze beneficiaries' decisions to access care, and so we aggregated all SADR visits on the same calendar day as one visit, and all TEDNI claims to the same provider on the same calendar day as one visit. We then constructed a variable for each beneficiary, in each month, to indicate whether the beneficiary had accessed any care from an MTF during the month, or from a civilian network provider during the month.

The left side of Figure 3.1 shows the results of the regression analysis of the likelihood that spouses of soldiers utilize outpatient care in a month, overall, and at MTFs and civilian providers. The chart shows the probability of using any outpatient care and the predicted change in that likelihood when the soldier in the household is deployed. We see that when the soldier was at home, spouses visited a provider in 48 percent of the months. Spouses visited MTF providers in 39 percent of the months, and network providers in 17 percent of the months. These

Figure 3.1
Likelihood of One or More Spouse Visits in a Month

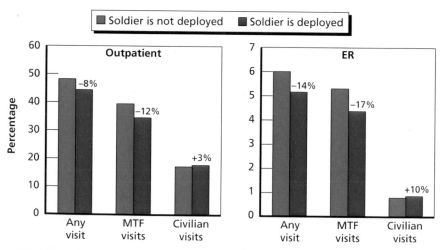

NOTE: All results significant at the 0.001 level.
RAND RR257-3.1

two totals do not sum to the general likelihood of 48 percent that a spouse visits a provider in a month, because a spouse may visit both an MTF provider and a civilian provider in the same month.

We see that spouses were less likely to visit MTF providers when the soldier in the household was deployed, and spouses were more likely to visit civilian providers when the soldier was deployed (Figure 3.1). However, MTF visits decreased in likelihood significantly more than network visits increased in likelihood, for a net decrease in spouse utilization when the soldier in the household was deployed.

We saw the same trend in ER utilization for spouses that we saw for general outpatient visits, except that the magnitude of the trend was larger. Spouses were less likely to visit ERs at MTFs, but more likely to visit civilian network ERs. Overall, spouses were less likely to visit ERs when the soldier in the household was deployed.

We found interesting the finding that civilian care increased for spouses while the total likelihood of using care decreased. We expected that the increase in civilian visits was caused by family members leaving the area around the MTF, and utilizing care where available from civilian providers. We tested this hypothesis by distinguishing civilian care provided in the 40-mile radius surrounding MTFs (or catchment area) from civilian care provided outside this radius. We observed a very large relative increase in the likelihood that spouses access care from civilian providers outside their catchment area (Figure 3.2). The increase is so large that it dominates a smaller decrease in the likelihood that spouses access network care within their catchment area.

During deployments, spouses' likelihood of utilizing outpatient care for mental health for mood, adjustment, and anxiety (MAA) diagnoses increased by 4 percent (Figure 3.3). Similar studies frequently utilize these three diagnoses as the notable diagnoses associated with stress and depression (Mansfield et al., 2010; Mansfield et al., 2011). Although small in magnitude, this increase in mental health utilization contrasts with the overall decline in spouse utilization during the deployment period.

Figure 3.2
Spouse Utilization of Outpatient Care from Civilian Providers

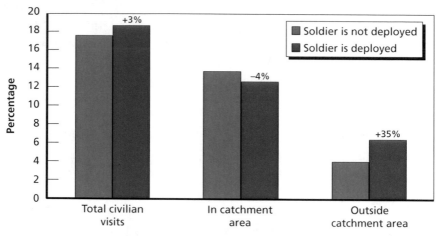

NOTE: All results significant at the 0.001 level.
RAND RR257-3.2

Figure 3.3
Likelihood of Spouse Mental Health Visit for Mood, Adjustment, and Anxiety

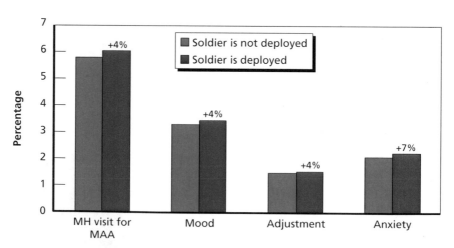

NOTE: All results significant at the 0.001 level.
RAND RR257-3.3

Changes in Child Health Care Utilization

We performed an analysis of child utilization of outpatient care, noting the change in child utilization from when the soldier in the household was at home compared to when the soldier was deployed. While spouses decreased outpatient utilization overall, children experienced little change in likelihood of using outpatient care and were slightly more likely to visit the ER. In Figure 3.4 we see a similar trend as we saw with spouses, where children shift use of outpatient care from MTF providers to civilian providers.

We see similar trends in the likelihood with which children visited the ER when the soldier in the household was at home or deployed, although MTF visits to the ER remain unchanged and civilian-provider MTF visits increase more greatly.

As we studied spouse utilization further to understand the extent to which the increase in network care occurred outside the beneficiaries' catchment areas, we performed the same analysis for children. We observed a similar result, shown in Figure 3.5, that children were more

Figure 3.4
Likelihood of Children Utilizing Outpatient Care in a Month

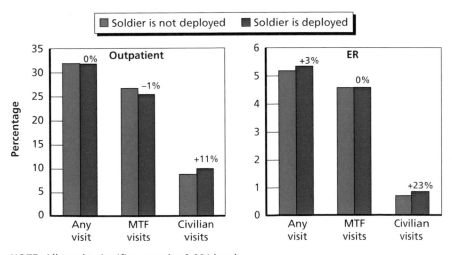

NOTE: All results significant at the 0.001 level.

RAND RR257-3.4

Figure 3.5
Likelihood of Children Utilizing Civilian Care in a Month

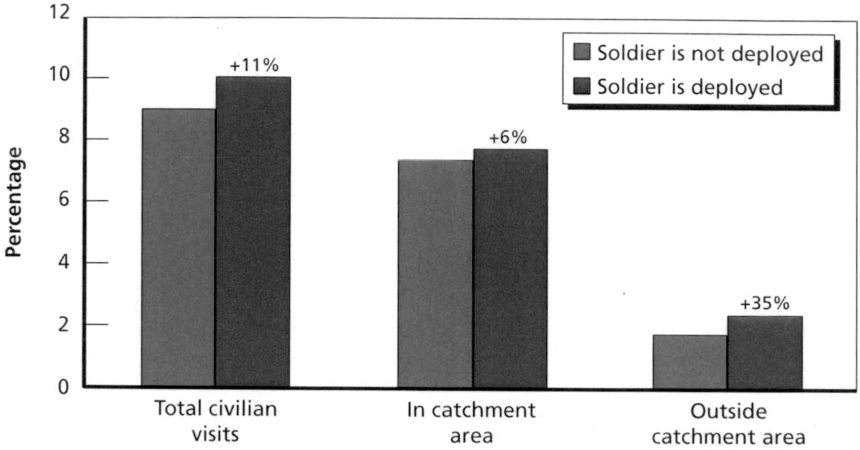

NOTE: All results significant at the 0.001 level.
RAND *RR257-3.5*

likely to utilize care outside their catchment area when a soldier in their immediate family was deployed.

We performed two additional analyses to gain further insight into the effect that soldier deployments had on children in Army families. We looked specifically at the effect of soldier deployments on the health care utilization by children of single parents, because these include children who were previously living in a household headed by the soldier and who must live with another adult custodian while the single-parent soldier is deployed. We attempted to distinguish between families where the soldier was the custodial parent. We assumed that soldiers were custodial parents when they had the same residential zip code as the child. We are uncertain about the extent to which this assumption was accurate, but we do see sizably greater deployment cycle effects in the cases we assumed were custodial.[2]

---

[2] Children of families with two parents remain the large majority of cases. To compare results for children of single-parent families to those for children of two-parent families, consider the results for all children. They closely resemble those for children of two-parent families.

In Figure 3.6 we see a decrease in the likelihood that children of single soldiers, either custodial or noncustodial parents, utilize outpatient care. We observe a large decrease in utilization of MTFs, and an increase in utilization of civilian providers. The likelihood that children of custodial single parents used outpatient care at an MTF when the soldier was deployed decreased by 26 percent relative to the likelihood of utilization when the soldier was at home. The likelihood that these children utilized outpatient care from a civilian provider increased as well, by 13 percent relative to the likelihood of utilization when the soldier was at home.

We used the same categories of mental health diagnoses from the spouse analysis to calculate deployment cycle effects on child mental health utilization. In Figure 3.7 we see that while children in the analysis were only 1 to 2 percent likely to utilize mental health care for stress-related diagnoses in a month, utilization increased by 16 percent. Children in this analysis were more likely to utilize mental health care for conduct- and attention-related diagnoses. Utilization of mental health care for these diagnoses also increased when soldiers deployed.

Figure 3.6
Likelihood of Children of Single Parents Utilizing Outpatient Care, Monthly

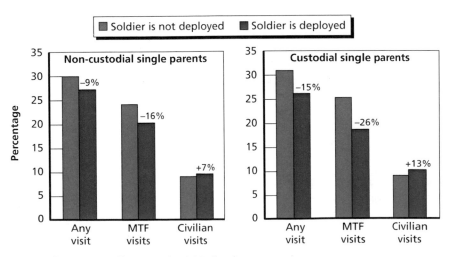

NOTE: All results significant at the 0.001 level.
RAND RR257-3.6

Figure 3.7
**Likelihood of Children Utilizing Mental Health Care for Stress-Related
Diagnoses in a Month**

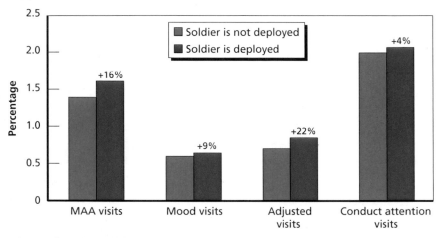

NOTES: All results significant at the 0.001 level.
RAND *RR257-3.7*

Spouse and Child Prescription Use

Finally, we looked at pharmaceutical utilization to see whether the
trends in this product line corroborated the findings in our general
analyses of outpatient, ER, and mental health utilization. We observed
that when a soldier was deployed, the likelihood of spouse prescription
use decreased slightly, by 7 percent, but the likelihood of antidepressant utilization increased by 7 percent (Figure 3.8).

For children, we found that the likelihood of any prescription use
increased slightly when the soldier in the household was deployed, by
1 percent, but we also found that the likelihood of antidepressant prescription use increased by 8 percent. Also notable, child anti-infective[3]
prescription use increased by 8 percent when soldiers deployed.

---

[3]   Anti-infective drugs include antibiotics.

Figure 3.8
Likelihood of Spouse and Child Prescription Use, Monthly

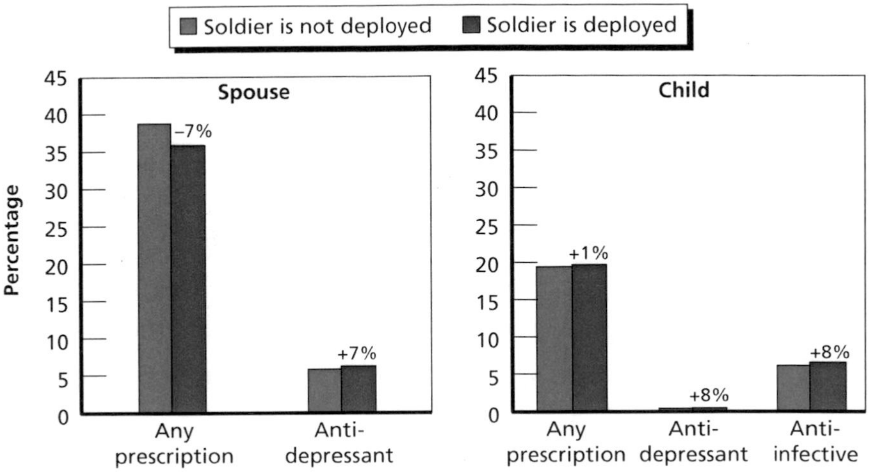

NOTE: All results significant at the 0.001 level.
RAND RR257-3.8

Deployment Cycle Effects on Newer Army Families

Through the course of performing the analysis we considered focusing specifically on newer Army families, to understand how deployment cycle events affected their health care utilization. We hypothesized that the population of Army families who had been in the Army for less time would be more affected by deployment cycle events, having had less experience managing the stresses of deployments and utilizing the TRICARE benefit and Army MTFs. We created a subset of the total population in the analysis (active component families enrolled in TRI-CARE Prime between 2004 and 2009), including only families of soldiers who entered the active component after 2001.

The population of "post-2001" families consisted of 151,000 spouses and 173,000 children, approximately half of the total beneficiaries in the analysis. The post-2001 population differed demographically from the whole: they were younger, they had been in the Army for less time, and the soldiers held lower rank. The average family size was

0.6 individuals smaller; spouse age was 25, compared to 31; the average child age was 4, compared to 7; the average soldier's time in service was 44 months, compared to 132; and 90 percent of these soldiers were enlisted, compared to 80 percent.

The deployment cycle effects on this population were consistent but larger, except that the effect of soldier deployments on family member mental health utilization was similar. We compare the magnitude of deployment cycle effects across the entire analysis population and the post-2001 population for the key analysis findings (Table 3.1).

Table 3.1
Comparison of Deployment Cycle Effects, Post-2001 Army Families

Deployment Cycle Effect	All Army Families	Post-2001 Families
Spouse MTF visits	−12%	−19%
Spouse civilian visits outside catchment area	+35%	+55%
Spouse mental health visits for stress-related diagnoses	+4%	+4%
Child MTF visits	−4%	−7%
Child MTF visits: children of single parents	−20%	−31%
Child civilian visits outside catchment area	+35%	+62%
Child mental health visits for stress-related diagnoses	+16%	+15%

Chapter Summary

Our longitudinal analysis of family members of deployed soldiers found the following:

Family members were generally less likely to utilize care when a soldier deploys from their family. Children of married parents experienced little change, but spouses and children of single soldiers were significantly less likely to utilize care.

All categories of family members were more likely to utilize civilian care when a soldier deployed from their family. During deployment, the likelihood of utilizing civilian care in the catchment area either increased slightly or decreased at a lesser rate than care from

MTFs. However, we observed a very large relative increase in likelihood that family members would utilize care from civilian providers outside their area while their soldier was deployed.

When soldiers deployed from the family, we saw increases in other health care utilization that is associated with populations under stress. Likelihood of ER visits by older children; mental health utilization by spouses for mood, adjustment, or anxiety; and spouse prescription fills for antidepressants all increased during deployment.

Deployment cycle effects are greater for newer Army families. These newer families are demographically distinct; they are younger and have been in the Army for less time, so they have less experience accessing health care through TRICARE, and they have smaller families. We expect that these demographic differences contribute to the amplified individual-level deployment cycle effects.

CHAPTER FOUR

Conclusions

This report describes how deployment cycle events affected the ability of MTFs to provide care to Army beneficiaries, as well as the aggregate change in care utilized by Army beneficiaries.

Soldier utilization decreases with deployments, but nondeploying soldiers use more care during these times. Several factors contribute to these effects: visits by nonenrolled soldiers, differences in utilization rates between soldiers in deployable and nondeployable units, and apparent changes in access for nondeploying soldiers during large deployments. However, further study would help the Army gain greater insight into the way its soldiers use health care, so it can better meet their needs in the future.

We conclude that MTF capacity is not greatly affected when soldiers deploy. In aggregate, family member access does not appear impinged when soldiers deploy, and MTFs may be slightly less busy overall. However, we caveat our conclusions with respect to the data available and recommend that if the Army seeks to better manage MTF capacity across the deployment cycle, further analysis will be useful concerning provider FTEs.

The deployment cycle affects installations differently. In our MTF analysis we focused on 14 force projection platforms in the United States. But even across these installations, the nature of soldier deployments varied. We chose a simple metric to differentiate installations that mainly deploy soldiers from installations that perform other missions, and observed substantial variance in maximum concurrent deployment across the installations in the analysis. The numerical methods we used in the MTF analysis functioned best when applied in aggregate, but we suggest that by understanding systemwide deployment cycle trends and tailoring analysis to individual installations, the Army can gain a rich understanding of how to manage changes to the beneficiary population and MTF capacity in the future.

Spouses and children of single parents decreased the amount of care they utilized when soldiers deployed. Although spouses decrease the total quantity of care they seek, they seek more mental health care for stress-related diagnoses when soldiers deploy from the household. This finding is consistent with the literature (e.g., Eide et al., 2010). Where we observe visits by children of single parents to decline dramatically when soldiers deploy, we do not know the extent to which need is unmet. While we are cautioned in prior research that deployments may negatively affect the well-being of children, and we might infer deployments to increase the children's need for health care, we know that these children are living with alternative caregivers and using more civilian care. It is possible that these children change their behaviors during these times to use care like nonmilitary households in the United States, at a lower rate than military households.

Family members who were enrolled to MTFs tended to shift their utilization to network providers from MTFs when soldiers deployed from the household, and were noticeably more likely to utilize care outside their area. Although we were unable to exhaustively assess the extent to which family members left the installation area when soldiers deployed, we take the measurable increase in utilization of civilian care outside the installation areas as an indication of this phenomenon.

We studied pharmaceutical utilization to corroborate our observations regarding outpatient care, and we saw a similar decrease in overall utilization. We observed exceptions, with a small increase in spouse use of antidepressants, which is expected when we observe a small increase in utilization of spouse mental health care.

Deployment cycle events affect newer families even more than the general Army population. Newer Army families in this analysis are younger, have less Army experience, and also have smaller families. In the areas where we observed some of the largest deployment cycle effects on individuals, dependents seeking care outside the installation area when soldiers deploy and effects on children of single parents, these effects are even larger for those newer families. Understanding the needs of these individuals further would help the Army ensure support for them.

Future studies may also consider soldiers and family members in the reserve components. They were excluded from our longitudinal analysis of family members, since we did not have data to study their health care utilization while not activated and thus ineligible for TRICARE. Additional analyses should also consider Army beneficiaries outside the United States, as TRICARE Overseas differs from TRICARE Prime, and these beneficiaries were excluded from the analysis.

References

Bowling, U.B., and M. Sherman, "Welcoming Them Home: Supporting Service Members and Their Families in Navigating the Tasks of Reintegration," *Professional Psychology Research and Practice*, Vol. 39, No. 4, 2008, pp. 451–458.

Chandra, A., L.T. Martin, S. Hawkins, and A. Richardson, "The Impact of Parental Deployment on Child Social and Emotional Functioning: Perspectives of School Staff," *Journal of Adolescent Health*, Vol. 46, No. 3, 2010a, pp. 218–223.

Chandra, A., S. Lara-Cinisomo, and L.H. Jaycox, et al., "Children on the Homefront: The Experience of Children from Military Families," *Pediatrics*, Vol. 125, No. 1, 2010b, pp. 16–25.

Chartrand, M.M., et al., "Effect of Parents' Wartime Deployment on the Behavior of Young Children in Military Families," *Archives of Pediatric and Adolescent Medicine*, Vol. 162, No. 11, 2008, pp. 1009–1014.

Doperak, Martin D., *A Comparison of Dependent Primary Care Utilization Rates Based on Deployments*, Office of the Surgeon General (Army), Falls Church, VA, March 9, 2009.

Eide, Matilda, Gregory Gorman, and Elizabeth Hisle-Gorman, "Effects of Parental Military Deployment on Pediatric Outpatient and Well-Child Visit Rates," *Pediatrics*, Vol. 126, No. 1, July 1, 2010, pp. 22–27.

Flake, E.M., et al., "The Psychosocial Effects of Deployment on Military Children," *Journal of Developmental and Behavioral Pediatrics*, Vol. 30, No. 4, 2009, pp. 271–278.

Gorman, Gregory H., Matilda Eide, and Elizabeth Hisle-Gorman, "Wartime Military Deployment and Increased Pediatric Mental and Behavioral Health Complaints," *Pediatrics*, Vol. 126, No. 6, December 1, 2010, pp. 1058–1066.

Headquarters, U.S. Army Medical Command, *Fragmentary Order (FRAGO) 12 to MEDCOM OPORD 04-01 (Support to OIF2 and OEF5 Supporting the Global War on Terrorism (GWOT)* (U), Fort Sam Houston, March 14, 2005. Not available to the general public.

Lyle, David S., "Using Military Deployments and Job Assignments to Estimate the Effect of Parental Absences and Household Relocations on Children's Academic Achievement," *Journal of Labor Economics*, Vol. 24, No. 2, April 2006, pp. 319–350.

Mansfield, Alyssa J., Jay S. Kaufman, Stephen W. Marshall, Bradley N. Gaynes, Joseph P. Morrissey, and Charles C. Engel, "Deployment and the Use of Mental Health Services Among U.S. Army Wives," *New England Journal of Medicine*, Vol. 362, January 14, 2010, pp. 101–109.

Mansfield, Alyssa J., Jay S. Kaufman, Charles C. Engel, and Bradley N. Gaynes, "Deployment and Mental Health Diagnoses Among Children of U.S. Army Personnel," *Archives of Pediatric and Adolescent Medicine*, Vol. 165, No. 11, 2011, pp. 999–1005.

McNulty, P.A., "Does Deployment Impact the Health Care Use of Military Families Stationed in Okinawa, Japan?" *Military Medicine*, Vol. 168, No. 6, June 2003, pp. 465–470.

Meara, Ellen R., Seth Richards, and David M. Cutler, "The Gap Gets Bigger: Changes in Mortality and Life Expectancy, by Education, 1981–2000," *Health Affairs*, Vol. 27, No. 2, 2008, pp. 350–360.

Richardson, Amy Frances, Anita Chandra, Laurie T. Martin, Claude Messan Setodji, Bryan W. Hallmark, Nancy F. Campbell, Stacy Hawkins, and Patrick Grady, *Effects of Soldiers' Deployment on Children's Academic Performance and Behavioral Health*, Santa Monica, Calif.: RAND Corporation, MG-1095-A, 2011. http://www.rand.org/pubs/monographs/MG1095.html

Sorbero, Melony E., Stuart S. Olmsted, Kristy Gonzalez Morganti, Rachel M. Burns, Ann C. Haas, and Kimberlie Biever, *Improving the Deployment of Army Health Care Professionals: An Evaluation of PROFIS*, Santa Monica, Calif.: RAND Corporation, TR-1227-A, 2013. http://www.rand.org/pubs/technical_reports/TR1227.html

White, C., H.T. de Burgh, N.T. Fear, and A.C. Iversen, "The Impact of Deployment to Iraq or Afghanistan on Military Children: A Review of the Literature," *International Review of Psychiatry*, Vol. 23, No. 2, 2011, pp. 210–217.